SAVING ENDANGERED SPECIES

THE
CALIFORNIA CONDOR
Help Save This Endangered Species!

Alison Imbriaco

MyReportLinks.com Books

an imprint of

Enslow Publishers, Inc.
Box 398, 40 Industrial Road
Berkeley Heights, NJ 07922
USA

MyReportLinks.com Books, an imprint of Enslow Publishers, Inc. MyReportLinks®
is a registered trademark of Enslow Publishers, Inc.

Library of Congress Cataloging-in-Publication Data

Imbriaco, Alison.
  The California condor: help save this endangered species! / Alison Imbriaco.
     p. cm. — (Saving endangered species)
  Includes bibliographical references and index.
  ISBN-13: 978-1-59845-043-9
  ISBN-10: 1-59845-043-3
  1. California condor—Juvenile literature. I. Title.
QL696.C53I43 2007
598.9'2—dc22
                                        2006023511

Printed in the United States of America

10 9 8 7 6 5 4 3 2 1

To Our Readers:
Through the purchase of this book, you and your library gain access to the Report Links that specifically
back up this book.
The Publisher will provide access to the Report Links that back up this book and will keep these Report
Links up to date on **www.myreportlinks.com** for five years from the book's first publication date.
We have done our best to make sure all Internet addresses in this book were active and appropriate when
we went to press. However, the author and the Publisher have no control over, and assume no liability
for, the material available on those Internet sites or on other Web sites they may link to.
The usage of the MyReportLinks.com Books Web site is subject to the terms and conditions stated on the
Usage Policy Statement on **www.myreportlinks.com**.
A password may be required to access the Report Links that back up this book. The password is found
on the bottom of page 4 of this book.
Any comments or suggestions can be sent by e-mail to comments@myreportlinks.com or to the address
on the back cover.

Photo Credits: © David Watkins/Shutterstock.com, p. 92; © Ferenc Cegledi/Shutterstock.com,
pp. 25, 78; © John Brooks/U.S. Fish and Wildlife Service, p. 65; © Josue Adib Cervantes
Garcia/Shutterstock.com, p. 90; © Kim Worrell/Shutterstock.com, p. 67; © Shutterstock.com, pp. 10,
27, 99; Arizona Game & Fish, p. 20; ARKive, p. 86; California Academy of Sciences, p. 106; California
Department of Fish & Game, p. 48; Center for Biological Diversity, p. 14; Cornell Lab of Ornithology,
p. 12; Defenders of Wildlife, p. 104; Ecology.info, p. 89; Enslow Publishers, Inc., p. 5; IUCN, p. 69;
MyReportLinks.com Books, p. 4; National Audubon Society, p. 52; National Park Service, p. 97; National
Parks Conservation Association, p. 57; National Public Radio, p. 44; National Wildlife Federation, p. 95;
NatureServe, p. 42; Northern Arizona University, p. 47; Oregon Zoo, p. 76; Raptor Center, University of
Minnesota, College of Veterinary Medicine, p. 102; Smithsonian National Zoological Park, p. 94; Stanford
University, p. 107; The Los Angeles Zoo, p. 16; The Peregrine Fund, p. 101; The Ventana Wildlife Society,
p. 36; U.S. Fish and Wildlife Service, 1, 3, 18, 21, 29, 30, 33, 34, 39, 51, 55, 59, 63, 71, 82, 84, 109,
112, 113, 115; U.S. House of Representatives, p. 23; University of Michigan, p. 80; Zoological Society of
San Diego, p. 73.

Cover Photo: U.S. Fish and Wildlife Service

CONTENTS

MyReportLinks.com Books
Great Books, Great Links, Great for Research!

The Internet sites featured in this book can save you hours of research time. These Internet sites—we call them "Report Links"—are constantly changing, but we keep them up to date on our Web site.

When you see this "Approved Web Site" logo, you will know that we are directing you to a great Internet site that will help you with your research.

Give it a try! Type http://www.myreportlinks.com into your browser, click on the series title and enter the password, then click on the book title, and scroll down to the Report Links listed for this book.

The Report Links will bring you to great source documents, photographs, and illustrations. MyReportLinks.com Books save you time, feature Report Links that are kept up to date, and make report writing easier than ever! A complete listing of the Report Links can be found on pages 116–117 at the back of the book.

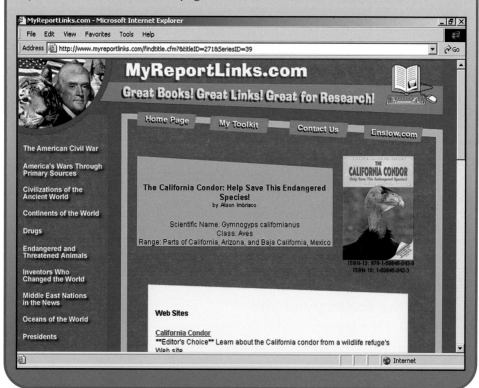

Please see "To Our Readers" on the copyright page for important information about this book, the MyReportLinks.com Web site, and the Report Links that back up this book.

Please enter **CCS1396** if asked for a password.

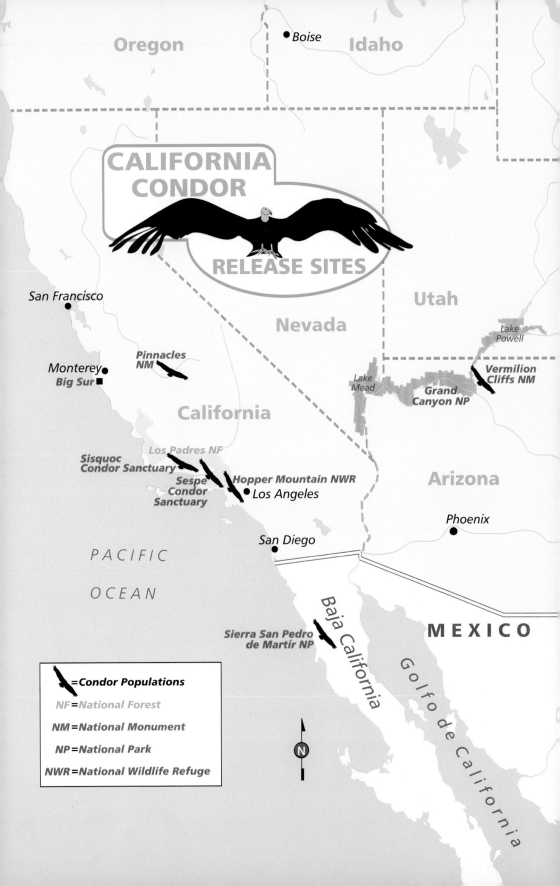

CALIFORNIA CONDOR FACTS

▶ **Scientific Name**
Gymnogyps californianus

▶ **Family**
Cathartidae (The word comes from the Greek word *kathartes,* which means "purifier.")

▶ **Habitat Needs**
Caves and cliff ledges for nest sites, high perches for roosting, open grasslands or open woodlands for finding food, winds or thermals for soaring

▶ **Size**
Length: 3.5 to 4.6 feet (1.1 to 1.4 meters)

Weight: 18 to 25 pounds (8.2 to 11.3 kilograms)

Wingspan: 9 to 10 feet (2.7 to 3 meters)

▶ **Condor Eggs**
Average size: 4.3 × 2.6 inches (109 × 66 millimeters)

Average weight: 9.4 ounces (266 grams)

Incubation time: 54 to more than 60 days

▶ **Age at First Flight**
About six months

▶ **Age at Maturity**
Six years

▶ **Life Span**
Unknown, but possibly up to sixty years

▶ **Date Listed**
The California condor was first listed on a federal list of endangered species in 1967, under the Endangered Species Preservation Act of 1966.

► Locations

Captive condors live at the San Diego Zoo's Wild Animal Park and the Los Angeles Zoo in California, the World Center for Wild Birds of Prey in Boise, Idaho, and the Oregon Zoo. Wild condors live in southern and central California, northwestern Arizona, and Baja California, Mexico.

► Current Population

As of January 2007, according to the Pinnacles Condor Program of the National Park Service, the total California condor population was 279: 152 in captivity and 127 in the wild. Of the birds in the wild, 70 were in California, 46 in Arizona, and 11 in Baja California, Mexico.

► California Condor Recovery Plan Goals

One captive population and two separate wild populations, each with at least one hundred fifty individuals and at least fifteen breeding pairs

► Threats

Lead poisoning, habitat destruction, collisions with power lines, shooting, and golden eagle and coyote predation of young chicks

In their mastery of the skies, condors outstrip all their fellow flying creatures. . . . Who amongst us has not yearned for condorlike abilities to sail through the air, silently surveying the forests and plains, moving long distances without a wingbeat, and landing at will on precipitous crags?

Noel and Helen Snyder, *The California Condor*

Chapter 1

A PREHISTORIC SURVIVOR IN MODERN TIMES

With a wingspan about one and a half times as long as a six-foot man is tall, the California condor is the largest bird in North America. It is hard to imagine a bigger bird, but forty thousand years ago, when the California condor was a relatively new species, it shared the sky with birds that were even larger.

▶ What Prehistoric Condors Saw

Scientists think a prehistoric bird named *Teratornis incredibilis* had wings that measured more than 17 feet (5.2 meters) from tip to tip. When this giant wanted to soar, it could just spread its great wings and let the wind lift it into the air. The bones of a smaller teratorn, *Teratornis merriami,* have been discovered in the La Brea Tar Pits in Rancho La Brea, Los Angeles, California. This bird had a wingspan one or two feet longer than that of the California condor.

Other bones taken from the asphalt at Rancho La Brea tell us what the California condors saw when they flew over North America thirty to forty

▲ California condors, the largest birds in North America, soar on wind currents when flying. A condor's wings measure more than nine feet from tip to tip.

thousand years ago. At that time, Columbian mammoths that stood more than twelve feet tall at the shoulder and weighed more than ten thousand pounds munched on grasses. Camels lived in California then, although these camels looked more like oversized llamas. The meat-eating animals of those times included huge short-faced bears, weighing as much as eighteen hundred pounds, and muscular saber-toothed cats. Scientists believe that condors probably soared over much of North America at the time, since condor bones have been found in New York and Florida.

All of these animals would have provided food for condors, because these large vultures are obligate scavengers. Condors are not hunters. Instead, they eat carrion, the remains of animals that have already died. Then, as now, condors followed smaller scavengers to the dead animals. Imagine how many scavengers could feast on a giant mammoth!

▶ Change

About ten thousand years ago, many of the large North American animals went extinct. Some scientists think the arrival of human hunters on the continent caused their extinction. Others think climate change caused them to disappear. Whatever the cause, condors could no longer find the huge carcasses that had been their dinner in the past.

When the large land mammals disappeared, some condors adapted to the new conditions by turning to mammals that live in the ocean. Instead of dead mammoths and camels, dead whales and sea lions provided meals for the condors. Scientists can tell what condors ate thousands of years ago by analyzing condor bones from various time periods. Higher levels of carbon in the bones indicate that the condors ate land mammals. Higher levels of nitrogen indicate a diet of mammals from the ocean.[1]

After the large land animals disappeared, California condors, for the most part, lived along

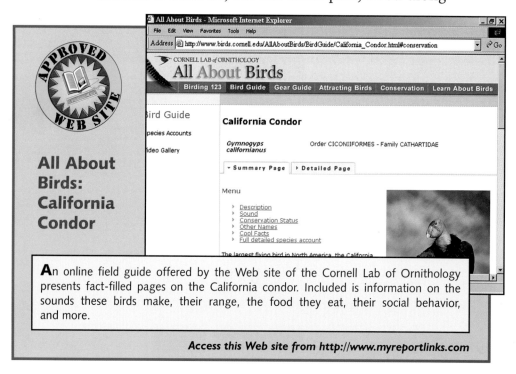

All About Birds: California Condor

An online field guide offered by the Web site of the Cornell Lab of Ornithology presents fact-filled pages on the California condor. Included is information on the sounds these birds make, their range, the food they eat, their social behavior, and more.

Access this Web site from http://www.myreportlinks.com

the Pacific coast, from British Columbia to Mexico. The ocean provided food, and the coastal mountain ranges provided nesting areas.

More Change

In the 1700s the landscape changed again when Europeans brought cattle to California. For a while, cattle ranching was big business in California. Cattle provided leather for shoemakers in the East, meat for eating, and fat for making the tallow used in candles. Herds of cattle rounded up for slaughter may have stretched a mile.[2] The remains of these cattle then provided food for the condors.

By the mid-1800s, cattle ranching began to become less important, but the discovery of gold in California led to a gold rush, bringing many more people. Many of these people were hunters, killing deer, elk, and other animals with lead bullets. Condors swallowed the carrion and in doing so, ingested some of the fragments of lead bullets. The lead entered the birds' bloodstream and paralyzed their digestive systems, so that the condors starved to death. Humans have since found how dangerous lead is not only to them but to all living creatures, which is why lead has been removed from paints, fuels, and other products that once contained it.

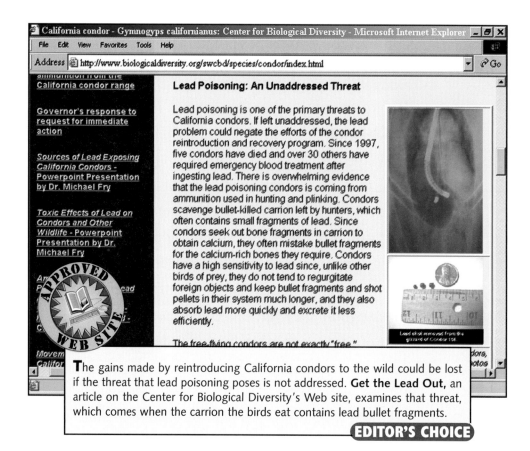

California condor - Gymnogyps californianus: Center for Biological Diversity - Microsoft Internet Explorer

File   Edit   View   Favorites   Tools   Help

Address http://www.biologicaldiversity.org/swcbd/species/condor/index.html

California condor range

Governor's response to request for immediate action

Sources of Lead Exposing California Condors - Powerpoint Presentation by Dr. Michael Fry

Toxic Effects of Lead on Condors and Other Wildlife - Powerpoint Presentation by Dr. Michael Fry

Lead Poisoning: An Unaddressed Threat

Lead poisoning is one of the primary threats to California condors. If left unaddressed, the lead problem could negate the efforts of the condor reintroduction and recovery program. Since 1997, five condors have died and over 30 others have required emergency blood treatment after ingesting lead. There is overwhelming evidence that the lead poisoning condors is coming from ammunition used in hunting and plinking. Condors scavenge bullet-killed carrion left by hunters, which often contains small fragments of lead. Since condors seek out bone fragments in carrion to obtain calcium, they often mistake bullet fragments for the calcium-rich bones they require. Condors have a high sensitivity to lead since, unlike other birds of prey, they do not tend to regurgitate foreign objects and keep bullet fragments and shot pellets in their system much longer, and they also absorb lead more quickly and excrete it less efficiently.

The free-flying condors are not exactly "free."

The gains made by reintroducing California condors to the wild could be lost if the threat that lead poisoning poses is not addressed. **Get the Lead Out,** an article on the Center for Biological Diversity's Web site, examines that threat, which comes when the carrion the birds eat contains lead bullet fragments.

EDITOR'S CHOICE

Condors disappeared from the Oregon coast during the mid-1800s. They left the southern portion of their range in the 1930s.[3] The condors' range became a wishbone-shaped area that extended along mountain ranges in six counties just north of Los Angeles in southern California.

▷ Preserving Condor Habitat

During the 1930s a deputy supervisor of the Los Padres National Forest named Cyril Robinson began the first thorough study of California condors. He noticed that a number of condors roosted in a part of the national forest around Sisquoc Falls. With the help of a local businessman and support from the National Audubon Society, he persuaded the United States Forest Service to establish the 1,200-acre (485-hectare) Sisquoc Condor Sanctuary. The sanctuary was the first area set aside for condors, and many more acres were preserved in the next decades.

The Forest Service set aside another 35,000 acres (14,165 hectares) in the Sespe region of the national forest in 1947. This Sespe Condor Sanctuary was later enlarged to include approximately 53,000 acres (twenty-one thousand hectares). In 1975 the U.S. Fish and Wildlife Service (FWS) purchased the nearby Hopper Ranch, which became the Hopper Mountain National Wildlife Refuge.

Protection for Condors

The California condor was included on the first federal list of endangered species in the United States in 1967. The species was one of the first to be covered by the Endangered Species Act, passed in 1973. Two years later, the California Condor Recovery Team was established, and a recovery plan for the species was adopted.

During the next decade, individuals with the recovery team, the National Audubon Society, and other conservation groups argued passionately about the best course of action to take to save the condor. Should condors be left alone in habitat set aside for them? Should radio transmitters be attached to their wings to help researchers study them? Should some of the birds be captured to begin a captive-breeding program? People who cared deeply about the condors could not agree about what to do. One of the main areas of disagreement was whether condors should be left alone in their sanctuaries or monitored to find out why they were dying.

In the meantime, the condor population was shrinking. By 1985, only six birds lived in the wild. By then, some condors lived at the Zoological Society of San Diego, more often referred to as

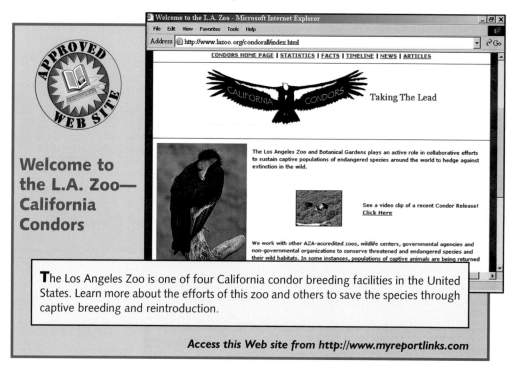

Welcome to the L.A. Zoo— California Condors

The Los Angeles Zoo is one of four California condor breeding facilities in the United States. Learn more about the efforts of this zoo and others to save the species through captive breeding and reintroduction.

Access this Web site from http://www.myreportlinks.com

the San Diego Zoo, and the Los Angeles Zoo. The captive population included an adult bird rescued in 1967, several young birds rescued as chicks, and thirteen chicks that had hatched from eggs taken from the wild. Because so many condors were dying in their habitat, the U.S. Fish and Wildlife Service authorized the recovery team to trap the remaining wild condors and bring them into captivity. The last wild condor was trapped in April 1987.

▶ Captive Breeding

From that low point in 1987, the number of living condors increased quickly. Zookeepers pushed captive condors to produce more eggs by removing the eggs as soon as they were laid. The condors would then lay replacement eggs, which were also removed. The eggs were hatched in incubators and protected in zoos, so their survival rate was much higher. Within twenty years, the condor population stood at 279 birds.[4]

▶ Condors in the Wild Again

In 1992, the California Condor Recovery Team began releasing young condors into the wild. The California Condor Recovery Plan calls for three separate condor populations, each numbering at least 150 individuals. One population would live in captivity; the other two would live in the wild, in areas separated by many miles to keep the populations apart. The plan calls for two separate wild populations to prevent all wild condors from being destroyed by a single natural catastrophe or disease.

In 1996, condors were released in Arizona, northwest of the Grand Canyon. Then, in 2002,

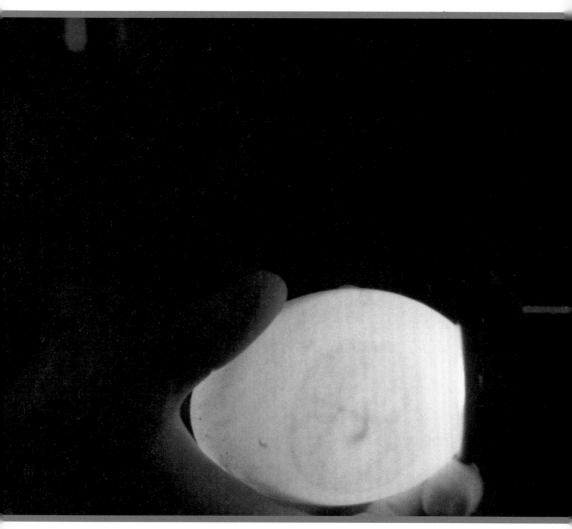

▲ A member of the California Condor Recovery Team candles a condor egg at the San Diego Zoo in 1998. In the candling process, a high-intensity light is shone through the egg to see how the embryo within is developing.

several young condors arrived in Baja California, Mexico, to begin a third population.

The Lead Problem

The condor population has increased quickly, but whether or not condors can survive in the wild is not certain. All of the condors in the wild are monitored by field biologists who track signals from devices attached to the condors' wings. The field biologists supply food for the condors, chase them away from populated areas so people will not feed them, capture them for blood samples, and take them in for treatment when the blood samples show high levels of lead. The main reason that condors in the wild are not yet wild condors is lead: Condors have shown that they can reproduce and survive on their own, but their food sources often contain lead. Recovery team members still need to provide them with safe food.

In the second half of the 1900s, recovery team members became convinced that something in the condors' habitat was causing them to die. Some scientists believe that the condors' habitat is just as dangerous today as it was in 1986.

The species has adapted to tremendous change through the many thousands of years it has been around, but it is possible that the changes brought by people will prove too much for this survivor.

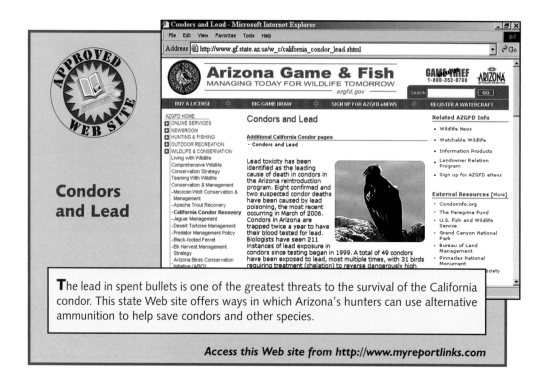

Condors and Lead

The lead in spent bullets is one of the greatest threats to the survival of the California condor. This state Web site offers ways in which Arizona's hunters can use alternative ammunition to help save condors and other species.

Access this Web site from http://www.myreportlinks.com

▶What You Can Do

The first step toward helping an endangered species is learning about it. You are already taking that first step as you read this book. You can learn more by following the links in this book to Web sites with information about California condors and their habitat. As you learn about condors and the people working to save them, share what you learn with your friends and family.

In the United States, endangered species are protected by the Endangered Species Act (ESA), signed into law in 1973. This important act includes penalties for people who harm an individual of an endangered species and provides protections for the species' habitat. The ESA also requires that steps be taken to help endangered species "recover," or increase in number. The U.S. Fish and Wildlife Service, part of the Department of the Interior, is the government agency responsible for bringing together experts to form a recovery team for each endangered species.

The ESA is often challenged by people who would like to use land that has been set aside for an endangered species. When Congress passed the act in 1973, the legislators made it clear that protection of endangered species might sometimes be more important than "improvements,"

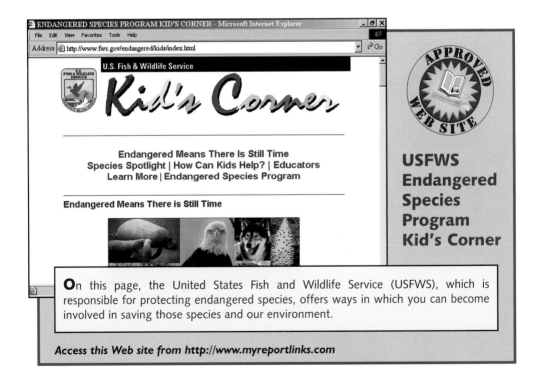

On this page, the United States Fish and Wildlife Service (USFWS), which is responsible for protecting endangered species, offers ways in which you can become involved in saving those species and our environment.

Access this Web site from http://www.myreportlinks.com

such as dams, that might benefit people. This decision was farsighted, but that kind of thinking is often unpopular.

Since endangered species depend on the protections provided by the ESA, find out more about this act and then explain to people how important it is. When you hear on the news about challenges to the ESA, write to your congressional representative to say how important the act is to you.

Knowledge Is Key

The presence of lead in carcasses is one of the greatest threats to the survival of California condors. A nontoxic alternative to lead bullets exists and is available to hunters. Learn more about the effects of spent lead bullets on many bird species. Then begin a campaign to educate hunters. They do not need to give up their sport; they need only replace their lead bullets with nontoxic bullets. Perhaps your class could design posters to put up in your community, or you might write a letter to the editor of your local newspaper to help educate people about the dangers that lead bullets or shot can pose.

If you live in California or visit the state on vacation, something as simple as picking up litter might help condors survive. Recently, biologists examined a wild condor chick that had died. They concluded that its death was caused by bottle caps

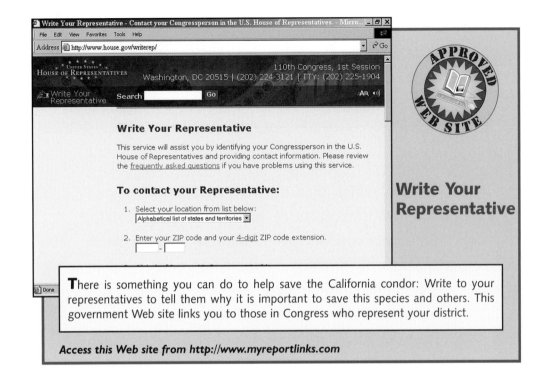

There is something you can do to help save the California condor: Write to your representatives to tell them why it is important to save this species and others. This government Web site links you to those in Congress who represent your district.

Access this Web site from http://www.myreportlinks.com

and pieces of plastic it had swallowed, because those items littered its nest cave. Adult condors and ravens may have brought the trash to the cave. Condor chicks, like other young animals, are very curious and will examine and sometimes swallow interesting-looking objects. It is also possible that the condor parents mistook the pieces of plastic for pieces of bone. Talk to your friends about how you can spread the word that littering is harmful to all living things: people, plants, and wildlife.

FLYING HIGH

With wings that measure about nine and a half feet (nearly three meters) from tip to tip, California condors are the largest birds in North America. By comparison, the wings of the whooping crane, another very large bird, span about seven feet (two meters). Golden eagles' wings measure about six and a half feet (nearly two meters) from tip to tip. When standing, condors are 45 to 55 inches (114 to 140 centimeters) tall.[1] They may weigh 20 pounds (9 kilograms) or more.

▷ Not Just Another Pretty Face

Not many people would describe condors as handsome or beautiful birds. One nature writer even described a condor's head as looking like "the survivor of a terrible fire."[2] It has no feathers except for a small patch of very short black feathers between the eyes. But those nearly hairless heads are beautiful in their function: The lack of feathers allows the condors to eat the rotting flesh of dead animals without having it stick to them. Adult condors' featherless heads and necks are usually pinkish-orange although the skin can

As the saying goes, beauty is in the eye of the beholder. If that is true, for those who have worked so hard to save the California condor from extinction, this bird is beautiful indeed.

become red, blue, purple, or bright yellow during a courtship display or other times when the birds are excited. When condors want to look threatening, they inflate air sacs to puff out the skin on their necks and cheeks. Condors do not have vocal cords, but they are able to hiss and grunt.

Unlike the males and females of many other bird species, male and female condors look so much alike that researchers have to take blood samples to discover a condor's sex. Most of an adult condor's feathers are black. White feathers on the underside of the wings form a long triangle, and silver or white feathers form a bar just above the long primary feathers on the upper side of the wings. A ruff of narrow straight feathers surrounds the condor's head.

Masters of Soaring Flight

As condors soar high above the ground, with wings spread and long primary feathers curved gracefully upward, their flight seems effortless. Even from a distance, experienced bird-watchers are able to recognize condors because their wings usually form a steady, straight horizontal line. The wings of turkey vultures, on the other hand, turn upward to form a shallow V and often wobble, dipping from side to side, as do the wings of smaller vultures. When condors come closer to people, the sound of the wind blowing through their feathers can be heard. The sound has been described as a "vaguely musical roar."[3]

Condors spread their wings to catch movement in the air, such as breezes from nearby mountains. They also take advantage of rising air currents called thermals, which result when ground-level temperatures increase and cause the air nearest the ground to rise. Condors use these rising air currents to circle upward, sometimes reaching heights of 15,000 feet (4,600 meters).[4] When looking for food, the huge birds glide lower, able

▲ A California condor in flight is an exhilarating sight to see. It can soar for hours in the sky without flapping its wings and reach speeds of up to fifty-five miles per hour.

to scan the ground beneath them with their keen eyesight.

Condors are masters of soaring flight, turning their long primary feathers to control speed and direction. Soaring near mountain ridges to catch the mountain breezes, condors can travel at 40 to 60 miles (64 to 97 kilometers) per hour. It is a good thing that they can soar because their large wings are not well suited for flapping. Condors usually flap their wings only during takeoffs and landings, although people have seen condors flap their wings while chasing golden eagles away from condor nests.[5]

▶ The Day of the Condor

Because condors rely on mountain winds and air thermals to fly, their flying time is limited by weather conditions. When weather is good, condors begin the day by sunning their wings, perhaps to dry any early morning dew. About midmorning, the condors take off to find food. Because they have chosen a high roost, they simply jump off, flap their wings a few times, and find an air current.

The five to six hours in the middle of the day provide the best conditions for flying. By early evening, the air often becomes still. Condors may fly 100 miles (160 kilometers) during the day, traveling near mountain ranges and foothills and scanning the ground below to find food.[6] Some days, particularly when the weather is bad, condors do not fly at all. Fortunately, they do not need to eat every day because when they do eat, they can consume up to 4 pounds (nearly 2 kilograms) of food at a time.

Finding Food

Since they do not have an especially good sense of smell, condors rely on their eyes for locating food. With their soaring flight, the huge birds can view many miles of landscape in a day. Researchers have noticed that condors often set off with a specific foraging area in mind. For example, during hunting season, condors fly to an area popular with deer hunters. During times when cattle are giving birth, condors fly over the ranches to look for stillborn calves.[7] Knowledge about where food can be found seems to be shared among condors and passed from generation to generation.

Appearances to the contrary, California condors take great care in grooming. After feasting on carrion, condors rub their heads and necks on rocks, grass, and branches to clean themselves.

For a condor, a good meal is an animal that has died recently. Condors are not predators—they do not kill animals for food. Unlike birds of prey, such as eagles, hawks, and owls, condors do not have sharp claws or talons and are therefore not able to grab and hold things with their feet. Instead, condors search for animals that are already dead. Anything from deer and cattle to squirrels and jackrabbits will do.

Condors often find a meal because other scavengers, such as coyotes, turkey vultures, or ravens, have already gathered there. When condors spot a

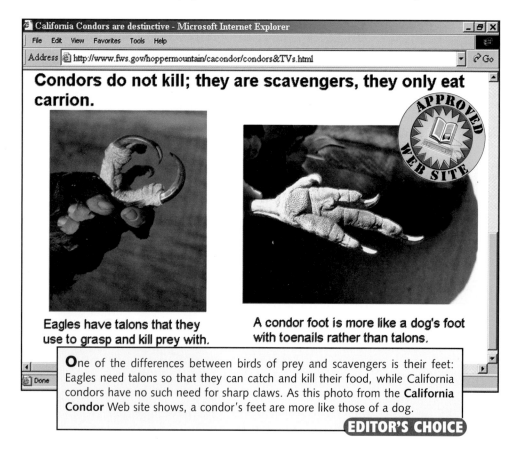

One of the differences between birds of prey and scavengers is their feet: Eagles need talons so that they can catch and kill their food, while California condors have no such need for sharp claws. As this photo from the **California Condor** Web site shows, a condor's feet are more like those of a dog.

EDITOR'S CHOICE

dead animal, they may circle the area for some time, perhaps signaling other condors that food has been found.[8] They then land on a tree or a rock to watch the other scavengers feeding.

This habit of watching others feed on a carcass before deciding to eat may be one that condors developed thousands of years ago when a saber-toothed cat might lie hidden, waiting to pounce on them. Today, few large predators are left. Sometimes the condors find golden eagles feeding on a carcass. The eagles do not like to share, and condors do not like the eagles' dangerous talons.

▶ Sharing Dinner

When the condors descend to a meal, with a loud rush of mighty wings to scare away smaller birds, they often eat communally, which means that a group of condors eat at the same time. The condors poke their heads inside the carcass and tear away chunks of meat with their razor-sharp beaks. They also look for small bones or pieces of bone that they can swallow. Bone provides much-needed calcium for the birds.

Condors eat from 1 to 4 pounds (.5 kilogram to 1.8 kilograms) at a time. Some of the food they swallow is stored in their crop, which is a pouch below the throat in the gullet, or esophagus. The food stored in the pouch might be fully digested later, or it might be used to feed condor chicks.

Having no feathers on their heads and necks means less of the dead animals' insides will stick to the condors as they poke their heads inside the carcass. Still, the birds rub their heads on grass or bushes after they eat to clean themselves. When they can, condors also splash in water to bathe.

Habitat

Condors prefer open countryside for finding food and rocky mountainsides for nests. In the twentieth century, before the last wild condors were brought into captivity, the wild condors' range was a wishbone-shaped area north of Los Angeles, California. At the bottom of the wishbone, the San Gabriel Mountains provided nesting areas. Along the sides of the wishbone, foothills and mountains along the San Joaquin Valley helped condors cruise the area, looking for carrion.

When the huge birds fly long distances, they stay close to the mountain ranges to take advantage of the mountain breezes. The air movements that condors need for flight are less reliable in flat country.

Family Life

At the age of six or seven, condors are old enough to look for mates and become parents. Condor courtship seems to begin with pair flights as two birds fly so close together they almost appear to be one large bird.[9] If both birds accept each other, the

As scavengers, condors do not need to kill prey for food: They leave that up to others. Instead they scan the ground far below and with keen eyes spot carrion there before swooping down to eat.

▲ *In this U.S. Fish and Wildlife Service photo, a California condor preens itself in the sun. After a courtship is established, condor partners will groom each other's feathers.*

relationship soon includes mutual preening: The birds stand close to one another and use their sharp beaks to clean each other's feathers and the skin on their heads. As the condors bond, males perform a dance in which they open their wings partway, droop their heads and necks, and lift their feet high in exaggerated steps as they circle the female.

Mated condors often stay together, roosting together at night and flying together to find food when one is not staying with an egg. Wild condors usually stay with a mate until one of them dies.

▶Nest Sites

In December, condor pairs begin to look for a good nest site.[10] If the pair has been together for a while, the condors will have their own territory with various nest sites, which include small caves in rocky cliffs and crevices in piles of boulders. Condors may also lay their eggs high in giant sequoia trees where fire has made large holes.

Condors do not build nests, although they may make a pad of dirt and gravel for the egg. Between January and March, the female condor lays one almost-white or pale greenish-blue egg, which is about 4.5 inches (110 millimeters) long and weighs about 10 ounces (280 grams).[11] The female and the male take turns brooding the egg, or keeping it warm with their body heat, by rolling the egg onto their feet and then resting on it so that the egg is surrounded by a brood patch of feathers on the adult's breast. The parents incubate the egg for about eight weeks, taking shifts of a day or more at a time. The brooding parent might leave the egg occasionally to drink from a nearby water source. The other parent flies by itself to find food. Sometimes a parent returning to take a brooding shift simply lands at the nest entrance and rolls the egg onto its feet. But sometimes both parents leave the egg briefly to soar together, leaving the egg untended.

If the floor of the cave or ledge is slanted, a condor parent getting up too quickly may cause the egg to roll. Biologists monitoring condors in 1982 watched an egg roll right out of a cave and smash onto rocks below.[12] Eggs in shallow caves or on ledges where other birds can see them are also at risk. Ravens watch for opportunities to get at condor eggs, break the shells, and eat them. Only about

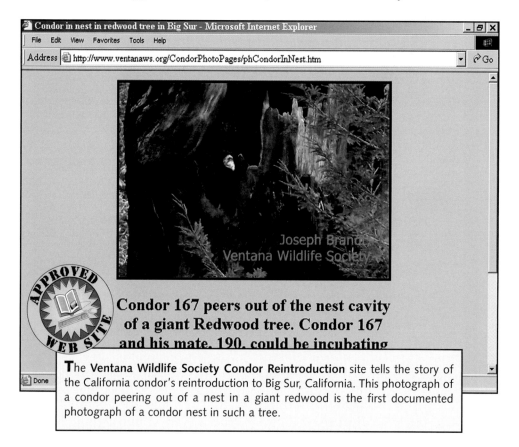

Condor in nest in redwood tree in Big Sur - Microsoft Internet Explorer

File   Edit   View   Favorites   Tools   Help

Address http://www.ventanaws.org/CondorPhotoPages/phCondorInNest.htm

Joseph Brandt,
Ventana Wildlife Society

Condor 167 peers out of the nest cavity of a giant Redwood tree. Condor 167 and his mate, 190, could be incubating

Done

The **Ventana Wildlife Society Condor Reintroduction** site tells the story of the California condor's reintroduction to Big Sur, California. This photograph of a condor peering out of a nest in a giant redwood is the first documented photograph of a condor nest in such a tree.

half of the condor eggs laid in the wild survive the long incubation period to produce chicks.

▶ Condor Chicks

It takes several days—sometimes almost a week—for a condor chick to hatch. Often, condor parents help the chick by carefully nibbling away bits of shell.

A just-hatched condor chick is covered with white down, except for its head, which is pale yellow-orange. Its parents continue to keep it warm by brooding it (covering it) just as they kept the egg warm. During the first week of the chick's life, the parents feed it every few hours.[13] The parents regurgitate, or bring up, food from their crops to their mouths, and the chicks put their heads inside the parent's mouth to eat.

When the chick is about two weeks old, its parents begin to leave it alone for longer periods of time and feed it less frequently. About a month after a chick has hatched, they may keep it warm only at night. Although the parents feed the chick less frequently as it grows, they continue to feed it for about a year.

After feeding sessions, the chick and its parent sit close to preen each other and rub their heads over each other's bodies.[14] Parents are not always gentle, though. Part of preparing a chick for the real world seems to include some rough treatment, including pecking at the chicks and dragging them.[15]

▶Growing Up

A chick's appearance begins to change a few weeks after it hatches. Gray down replaces the white down on its body. Later, gray down grows on the chick's head and neck as well. At about two months of age, the chick grows gray feathers, and the skin on its head turns dark gray.

As chicks spend more time alone, they play inside the nest area. When biologists watched wild condors in the early 1980s, they observed chicks jumping and spinning, flapping their wings, and digging in the floor of the nest area.[16] At about six weeks of age, chicks venture outside the nest area if they can. Sometimes, nest areas are caves in steep cliffs, and chicks cannot go far without falling. In fact, chicks are sometimes injured or killed when they fall as they attempt to explore their surroundings.

Condor chicks are very curious, and they play by tossing and chasing sticks and feathers. They may flap their wings vigorously as they attack a clump of sagebrush. Sometimes their wing flapping gets them airborne for a few minutes, but their first real fledge, or flight, will not happen until they are about six months old. During the months when condor chicks explore their

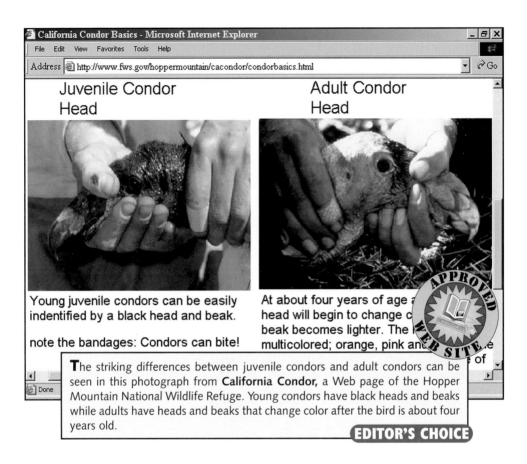

Juvenile Condor Head

Young juvenile condors can be easily indentified by a black head and beak.

note the bandages: Condors can bite!

Adult Condor Head

At about four years of age head will begin to change c beak becomes lighter. The multicolored; orange, pink an of

The striking differences between juvenile condors and adult condors can be seen in this photograph from **California Condor,** a Web page of the Hopper Mountain National Wildlife Refuge. Young condors have black heads and beaks while adults have heads and beaks that change color after the bird is about four years old.

EDITOR'S CHOICE

surroundings on foot, they are vulnerable to predators such as golden eagles and coyotes.

▶ Learning to Fly

First flights are short and clumsy. Landings, especially, take quite a bit of practice. Condors prefer to roost on dead tree branches or rocky cliffs so that they can fly away with just a few flaps of their giant wings. Landing on these perches takes a lot of skill.

Young condors practice flying close to home until they are about a year old and experienced enough to accompany their parents on the long flights to find food. They learn from their parents how to find food, where to look for it, and how to watch other scavengers feed before they risk burying their heads in a carcass.

On Their Own

Because condor parents usually spend more than a year raising a chick, they may not lay an egg every year. When they do prepare to lay another egg, they drive the older offspring away. The young condor will not be completely alone, though. By then it is part of condor society and can follow older condors to learn from them. Wildlife experts who study condors have observed what seem to be friendships among the birds, as two or more condors often roost together at night and fly together to look for food.

A young condor's appearance changes as it grows. When it is about three or four years old, its dark gray head begins to turn yellow, and white triangles gradually form under its wings. At the age of five or six, the young condor looks like an adult. It may live in the wild for as long as sixty years, although scientists have not been able to track this yet.

Chapter 3

A DANGEROUS ENVIRONMENT

From the earliest times, humans and human activities have caused condors to die. Long before European settlers arrived on the continent, American Indians from Oregon to southern California watched the magnificent soaring flight of the birds now called California condors. To them, condors were thunderbirds with magic powers. Because they believed the birds had the power to cause thunder and lightning, native peoples included condors in ceremonies. Often the ceremonies required the condors' death. Archaeologists studying remains of ancient native villages have found condor bones that are at least nine thousand years old.[1]

No one knows how many condors died in ceremonial rituals, but the number was probably large. The West Coast was home to many small tribes. If only some tribes sacrificed a thunderbird each year, the rituals might have meant the death of a hundred condors a year.[2]

Image Report Species - Gymnogyps californianus - Microsoft Internet Explorer

File Edit View Favorites Tools Help

Address http://www.natureserve.org/explorer/servlet/NatureServe?sourceTemplate=species_RptComprehensive.wi Go

Done

A California condor about to leave its perch is one of the photographs featured on the **NatureServe Explorer:** *Gymnogyps californianus* Web page. NatureServe is a conservation group that provides information about rare and endangered species.

▶Arrival of Europeans

When explorers and settlers of European descent arrived in condor territory, the killing of condors increased. As early as 1792, a man shot a California condor in Monterey, California. This bird, now stuffed, is still in the British Museum.[3] In 1805, a man traveling with the explorers Lewis and Clark killed a condor that was feeding on a dead whale. During the decades that followed, many more condors lost their lives simply because someone was curious about them.

The arrival of the dead condor at the British Museum inspired museum curators in Europe and the United States to offer payment for specimens of their own.[4] Scientists also wanted condor specimens to study. In the 1970s, a researcher with the U.S. Fish and Wildlife condor program decided to find out how many condors had lost their lives to scientific research. After studying records kept by collectors, scientific journals, and other old accounts, he found evidence of 300 condors that had died since 1792. That total included 177 condors killed by collectors.[5]

Early Threats to the Birds

In the mid-1800s, with the California gold rush, prospectors began using condor feathers to carry and measure gold dust. The primary feathers on the outside edge of condor wings are more than a foot long, and the quill is translucent so that people could see how much gold it contained. Some condors lost their lives so that prospectors could make use of the birds' feathers.

Other condors never got the chance to hatch from their eggs. Egg collecting was a popular hobby in the late 1800s and early 1900s, and the rare condor eggs were coveted by collectors. Egg collection may not have significantly affected the total condor population, though. Scientists later learned that condors that lose an egg early in the

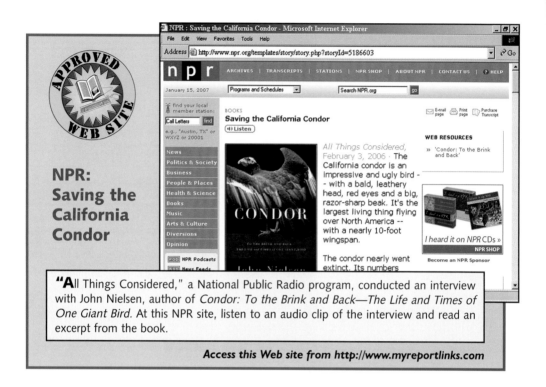

NPR:
Saving the
California
Condor

NPR : Saving the California Condor - Microsoft Internet Explorer

File   Edit   View   Favorites   Tools   Help

Address   http://www.npr.org/templates/story/story.php?storyId=5186603   Go

ARCHIVES | TRANSCRIPTS | STATIONS | NPR SHOP | ABOUT NPR | CONTACT US | ? HELP

January 15, 2007   Programs and Schedules   Search NPR.org   go

find your local
member station:
Call Letters   find
e.g., "Austin, TX" or
WXYZ or 20001

News
Politics & Society
Business
People & Places
Health & Science
Books
Music
Arts & Culture
Diversions
Opinion

NPR Podcasts
News Feeds

BOOKS
Saving the California Condor
Listen

CONDOR

TO THE BRINK AND BACK
THE LIFE AND TIMES OF ONE GIANT BIRD

John Nielsen

All Things Considered,
February 3, 2006 · The
California condor is an
impressive and ugly bird -
- with a bald, leathery
head, red eyes and a big,
razor-sharp beak. It's the
largest living thing flying
over North America --
with a nearly 10-foot
wingspan.

The condor nearly went
extinct. Its numbers

E-mail page   Print page   Purchase Transcript

WEB RESOURCES

» 'Condor: To the Brink
and Back'

I heard it on NPR CDs »
NPR SHOP

Become an NPR Sponsor

"All Things Considered," a National Public Radio program, conducted an interview with John Nielsen, author of *Condor: To the Brink and Back—The Life and Times of One Giant Bird.* At this NPR site, listen to an audio clip of the interview and read an excerpt from the book.

Access this Web site from http://www.myreportlinks.com

season can lay a replacement egg within a relatively short period of time.

Some condors were taken from the wild to be pets. While very large vultures may seem to be an unusual choice for a pet, condors are intelligent and social birds with distinct personalities. Owning condors was popular enough that records of these pets span more than fifty years.[6]

▷ Lead Poisoning

Most wildlife experts believe that the most serious threat to condors are the bullets aimed at other animals. It was not until the 1980s that scientists realized that condors are especially susceptible to lead poisoning after swallowing bullet fragments when they feed on animals killed by guns. Bullets are designed to explode on impact, which means that the carcasses of animals shot by hunters contain many pieces of lead.

Deadly Carcasses

Sometimes hunters shoot an animal and then are not able to find it. Ravens, coyotes, and other scavengers are better at finding dead animals than human hunters are. The scavengers then attract the attention of condors. Ranchers and other landowners sometimes kill animals they consider pests, such as coyotes and ground squirrels, and make no effort to remove or bury the body.

As condors feed on the carcasses, they swallow pieces of lead. Sometimes the lead fragments are too small to see. Condors may swallow larger pieces of lead on purpose, seeing them as bone fragments.[7] (Condors need the calcium in bone fragments to produce eggs.)

Not only are condors likely to swallow lead, but their digestive systems also try to digest it. Other scavengers more readily regurgitate, or throw up, what they cannot digest, but condors regurgitate less. They do often regurgitate fur, and many condor pellets have been found containing undigested material, but their stomach acids digest the lead they have eaten. As the lead enters their blood, the poison paralyzes the condors' digestive systems. Eventually they die of starvation even though their crops are full of food.

Environmental Hazards

Condors may have died from other forms of poison left behind by humans. During the late 1800s and early 1900s, ranchers and employees of the U.S. Fish and Wildlife Service put out meat poisoned with strychnine to kill predators, such as wolves and coyotes. Although scientists have no way of knowing how many condors may have died from eating the poisoned meat, some scientists believe the poison did kill some condors.

More recent human activities have also proven to be fatal to condors. Recently released young condors have died after flying into power lines. Others have been electrocuted when they perched on poles. One condor died after drinking from a puddle of antifreeze drained from someone's car.

Predators

Humans are not the only threat to condor survival. Predators view condor eggs and chicks as tasty meals. Ravens break condor eggs when they can and eat them. Unfortunately, condor parents sometimes leave their eggs long enough for ravens to get them.

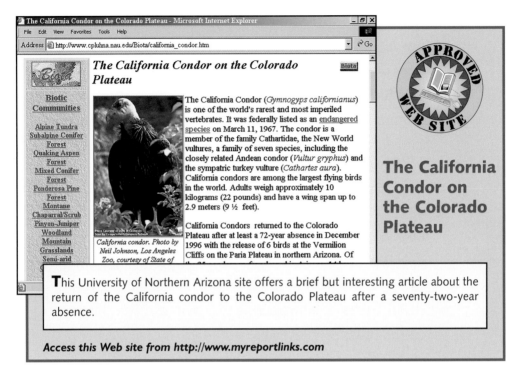

The California Condor on the Colorado Plateau

Biota

Biotic Communities

Alpine Tundra
Subalpine Conifer Forest
Quaking Aspen Forest
Mixed Conifer Forest
Ponderosa Pine Forest
Montane Chaparral/Scrub
Pinyon-Juniper Woodland
Mountain Grasslands
Semi-arid

The California Condor (*Gymnogyps californianus*) is one of the world's rarest and most imperiled vertebrates. It was federally listed as an endangered species on March 11, 1967. The condor is a member of the family Cathartidae, the New World vultures, a family of seven species, including the closely related Andean condor (*Vultur gryphus*) and the sympatric turkey vulture (*Cathartes aura*). California condors are among the largest flying birds in the world. Adults weigh approximately 10 kilograms (22 pounds) and have a wing span up to 2.9 meters (9 ½ feet).

California Condors returned to the Colorado Plateau after at least a 72-year absence in December 1996 with the release of 6 birds at the Vermilion Cliffs on the Paria Plateau in northern Arizona. Of

California condor. Photo by Neil Johnson, Los Angeles Zoo, courtesy of State of

The California Condor on the Colorado Plateau

This University of Northern Arizona site offers a brief but interesting article about the return of the California condor to the Colorado Plateau after a seventy-two-year absence.

Access this Web site from http://www.myreportlinks.com

Golden eagles and coyotes watch for a chance to snatch condor chicks as the young birds explore their surroundings. From the age of about six weeks until they learn to fly at about six months, curious young condors are often alone and vulnerable to predators. As the California Condor Recovery Team watched condors during the early 1980s, a team member witnessed two instances of eagles about to snatch chicks. In both cases, the condor parents were close by and chased the eagles away.[8]

▶ Slow Reproduction

Condors lay only one egg at a time and then spend a year or more taking care of their young. Because raising a young condor takes so long, condors do not lay eggs every year. In many cases, young condors do not survive to adulthood. One researcher calculated that when only about 50 percent of attempts to hatch and raise young are successful, the species cannot survive if more than 9 percent of the adult population dies per year.[9]

▶ Loss of Habitat

Like nearly every other endangered species, condors are threatened by loss of habitat. Condors prefer remote and rugged countryside, but even these areas are attractive to miners. The huge cattle ranches that once supplied large areas of open space and food for the condors have almost

California's Plants and Animals: California Condor

This Web page of the California Department of Fish & Game presents a historical overview of the California condor including milestones in the fight to save the species from extinction.

Access this Web site from http://www.myreportlinks.com

disappeared. Residential communities have replaced the ranches.

As early as the 1930s, the National Audubon Society began lobbying the federal government on behalf of the condors and their habitat. Thanks to the society's efforts and those of other conservation groups, remote mountain areas in California have been set aside for the condor.

Disease

California condors have strong immune systems. Without them, they would not be able to eat carrion and all the bacteria it contains without getting sick. However, the condors are susceptible to some diseases. In 2005, one chick born in the wild died from West Nile virus, spread by mosquitoes. Captive and wild California condors receive vaccinations to protect them from the disease, but the chick was so young that it had not yet been vaccinated.[10]

Efforts to Save the California Condor

Little was known about California condors before the 1900s. Although early explorers, pioneers, and scientists told stories about seeing the birds, no one studied them. Some of the condor stories were true, but others told of condors that carried off lambs and pets.[1]

▶ Early Condor Studies

In 1906, William Finley, an early conservationist and photographer, found a condor nest just as a chick was hatching and decided to document its development on film. There were no video cameras in 1906, and the equipment needed to take black-and-white photographs was large and cumbersome. Again and again, Finley and a friend hauled such equipment up a steep mountainside to take more than two hundred fifty photographs of the condor parents and chick. Finley's pictures indicate that the birds allowed the photographer to get quite close to them.

Eventually, Finley took the young condor home with him and named it General. After some time

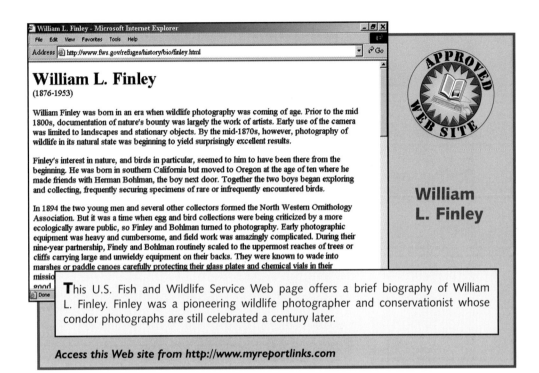

William
L. Finley

William L. Finley
(1876-1953)

William Finley was born in an era when wildlife photography was coming of age. Prior to the mid 1800s, documentation of nature's bounty was largely the work of artists. Early use of the camera was limited to landscapes and stationary objects. By the mid-1870s, however, photography of wildlife in its natural state was beginning to yield surprisingly excellent results.

Finley's interest in nature, and birds in particular, seemed to him to have been there from the beginning. He was born in southern California but moved to Oregon at the age of ten where he made friends with Herman Bohlman, the boy next door. Together the two boys began exploring and collecting, frequently securing specimens of rare or infrequently encountered birds.

In 1894 the two young men and several other collectors formed the North Western Ornithology Association. But it was a time when egg and bird collections were being criticized by a more ecologically aware public, so Finley and Bohlman turned to photography. Early photographic equipment was heavy and cumbersome, and field work was amazingly complicated. During their nine-year partnership, Finely and Bohlman routinely scaled to the uppermost reaches of trees or cliffs carrying large and unwieldy equipment on their backs. They were known to wade into marshes or paddle canoes carefully protecting their glass plates and chemical vials in their mission

This U.S. Fish and Wildlife Service Web page offers a brief biography of William L. Finley. Finley was a pioneering wildlife photographer and conservationist whose condor photographs are still celebrated a century later.

Access this Web site from http://www.myreportlinks.com

at Finley's home, General went to the Bronx Zoo where he lived for eight years. He died, unfortunately, after swallowing a rubber band.

Early pioneers in condor preservation also included Cyril Robinson. Robinson, a deputy supervisor of the Los Padres National Forest in central and southern California, did a study of condors during the 1930s that led to the establishment of the Sisquoc Condor Sanctuary in 1937.

▶ Carl Koford

The National Audubon Society sponsored a thorough study of condors that was begun in 1939 by Carl Koford, then a graduate student at the

University of California, Berkeley. During his four years of condor research, Koford often worked by himself and on foot, hiking steep mountainsides to view condor nests. Between 1939 and 1941, he spent about four hundred days watching the giant birds. Koford interrupted his research to serve in the U.S. Navy during World War II and then returned to the condors' wilderness area to spend another ninety-five days observing them. He filled thirty-five hundred pages of notes using a fine-point pen and small, careful penmanship.[2]

Koford's research consisted mostly of his observation of several condor pairs. He watched one pair hatch and raise a chick, which he named

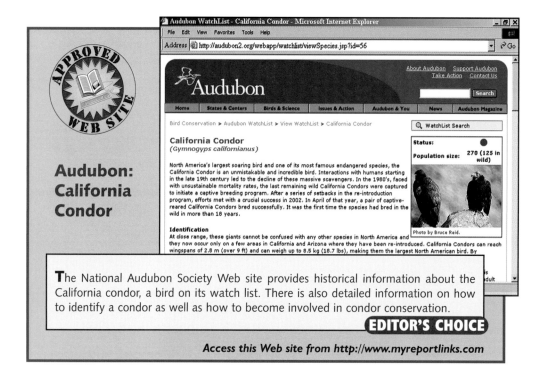

Audubon: California Condor

The National Audubon Society Web site provides historical information about the California condor, a bird on its watch list. There is also detailed information on how to identify a condor as well as how to become involved in condor conservation.

EDITOR'S CHOICE

Access this Web site from http://www.myreportlinks.com

Oscar. Sometimes he went into caves to examine eggs and chicks.

The researcher's thorough study of the condors was important in terms of condor conservation. Not only did he provide extensive information about condor nesting and parenting, but his research also showed that condors were in danger of becoming extinct. Using his research, the National Audubon Society persuaded the federal government to establish the Sespe Condor Sanctuary in 1947 to protect the area of Koford's study.

▶ Koford's Conclusions

In 1953, the National Audubon Society published Koford's research on condors. Two of the findings, however, were to become the source of heated debates about how best to preserve the species.

The first of Koford's controversial conclusions was that any human disturbance to the condors, even taking photographs of the birds, was harmful to them. During his study of condors, Koford went into nest sites to examine eggs and chicks, but by the end of his research, he had concluded that any human presence might cause extinction of the condor. He believed that helping condors survive meant giving them space and then leaving them completely alone. Koford's conclusion was that a hands-off approach was best. Based on that conclusion, conservationists put their energy into pressing the federal and state governments to set aside more wilderness for them.

A Question of Numbers

Koford's study contained a second conclusion that caused confusion and may have delayed further research. The published study estimated there were sixty condors alive in the mid-1940s. When an employee of the California Department of Fish and Game mentioned to Koford that he had seen eighty-five condors feeding together, Koford ignored the information, which did not agree with his estimate of the condor population.[3] Decades later, other researchers estimated that there were actually about one hundred fifty condors in the mid-1940s.

Koford's estimate made it difficult for later researchers to chart the steep decline in condor numbers. When population surveys of the condors late in the 1960s totaled about sixty condors, some officials argued that the species' population was stable even though people were seeing fewer condors in the sky.[4] If there were sixty condors in the 1940s and sixty condors in the 1960s, then the condors seemed to be holding their own. However, if there were one hundred fifty condors in the 1940s and sixty condors in the 1960s, the species was quickly headed toward extinction.

The problem was that at the time, it was not possible to get an accurate count of condors. People could not tell one bird from another as the birds flew overhead. In addition, condors often fly 100 miles in a day to find food. In a wilderness area with only a few dirt roads, people could not track the condors as they soared along rugged mountains.

▲ Observe the triangular white patches under the wings of this California condor in flight. By catching thermal air currents, condors can soar for hours.

First Captive-Breeding Effort

In 1952, a year before Koford's research was published, the San Diego Zoo asked the California Department of Fish and Game for a permit to capture two young condors to begin a captive-breeding program. The zoo received its permit, but the young condors were never captured.

As a trapper tried unsuccessfully to trap condors, conservationists who believed in a hands-off approach protested the permits. The National Audubon Society and other conservation groups argued that not enough was known about captive breeding of California condors. In addition, they said that breeding pairs might be separated and that the process of trapping condors to find suitable male and female birds might cause injury to birds.[5] The California Department of Fish and Game revoked the zoo's permits.

More Studies

During the 1960s, several studies of condors reached different conclusions. One study funded by the National Audubon Society and the National Geographic Society concluded that condors were being deliberately shot and accidentally poisoned when they ate the carcasses of poisoned coyotes. The report recommended that condors receive more federal protection, including a full-time warden to patrol the sanctuary. It also recommended that more effort be directed toward educating the public about condors. The National Audubon Society responded by providing a condor warden and by publishing information and giving talks to the public. In 1965, the National Audubon Society worked with the California Department of Fish and Game to organize annual counts of condors.

Two later studies by biologists with the U.S. Fish and Wildlife Service concluded that condors were laying fewer eggs and that condors might not be finding enough to eat. Ranchers in central California were selling their ranches, and fewer cattle grazed in condor foraging areas. The FWS biologists began putting out fresh animal

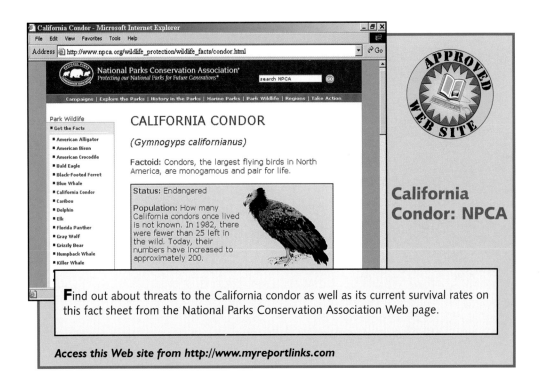

Find out about threats to the California condor as well as its current survival rates on this fact sheet from the National Parks Conservation Association Web page.

Access this Web site from http://www.myreportlinks.com

carcasses for the condors. The condors did take advantage of the extra meals, but they never became dependent on them.[6]

The Endangered Species Act

In 1973, Congress passed the important Endangered Species Act. The ESA states clearly that protection of endangered species should be a national priority. The act includes penalties for killing or harming an individual bird, animal, or plant of a species considered in danger of going extinct.

In addition, the ESA requires that steps be taken to help endangered species recover, or increase in numbers. The Department of the Interior is responsible for bringing together experts to form a recovery team for each endangered species. The California condors were among the first species to be studied as specified by the act.

The first California Condor Recovery Plan was approved in 1975. It emphasized protection of condor habitat. A year later the recovery team prepared a contingency plan, a plan to fall back on if the initial plan did not succeed, that recommended captive breeding. In 1976 the U.S. Fish and Wildlife Service designated about 570,400 acres (231,000 hectares) of land in six southern California counties as critical habitat for the condor, meaning those lands would be protected.[7]

▷ Disappearing Condors

In 1978, FWS biologists estimated that only 25 to 35 condors still lived in the wild. The condors were disappearing, but even after all the studies, no one knew why. Was it because condors were producing fewer chicks? Were the poisons used to kill coyotes and ground squirrels also killing condors? Or were habitat loss and less available

△ *A captive Andean condor at the Patuxent Wildlife Research Center in Maryland is watched closely by a Fish and Wildlife Service biologist in 2002. Research done on Andean condors there has played a pivotal role in the recovery of California condors.*

food the major problems? Few dead condors were ever recovered, so scientists seldom had opportunities to examine the birds to see why individuals had died.

California Condor Recovery Begins

In 1980 the California Condor Recovery Team applied to the California Department of Fish and Game for permits to begin a limited hands-on recovery effort. Believing that public opinion was against its plan, the recovery team chose to limit its requests. The California Department of Fish and Game granted permits to trap ten condors and put radio transmitters on them and to trap a young female to provide a mate for Topa Topa, a sick young condor that had been taken to the Los Angeles Zoo in 1967. Permission to take blood samples of the condors they trapped was denied, however.

Before recovery team members trapped a condor, they proceeded with the kind of research that earlier researchers had done before. They found condor nest sites and went into the caves to examine the chicks. The second chick that team members examined died from the stress of be-ing handled. The California Department of Fish and Game immediately canceled the permits that would have allowed the team to trap condors and put radio transmitters on them. Without the permits, the recovery team could only watch condors to learn more about them. The team did learn two important facts from their observations, however.

Discoveries

As team members watched condor nests, they noticed that if something happened to a condor egg early in the season (in February, for example), the condor pair would produce another one. This process of laying an egg to replace a lost egg is called double-clutching. No one had known for sure that condors would double-clutch, and learning that they did was a breakthrough for the recovery team. The fact that the condors replaced lost eggs meant that researchers could take eggs from condor nests without reducing the number of wild condors. The eggs taken from the nests would then be hatched in incubators.

The recovery team also discovered a way to tell one condor from another as the birds flew overhead. Photographs of condor wings showed differences in the long primary feathers. Researchers and volunteers began snapping pictures of condors whenever they saw them, and the recovery team soon had hundreds of photographs of the condors' great black wings against blue sky.

In 1982, more-sophisticated cameras made the first accurate count of condors possible, but with advanced technology came a sobering discovery: The recovery team researchers learned that only twenty-one condors were alive in the wild. By 1984, the number had dropped to fifteen.[8]

A Change of Direction

Knowledge that the total wild condor population consisted of only twenty-one birds at the end of 1982 spurred the California Department of Fish and Game to change its mind. It permitted the recovery team to trap condors so that small radio transmitters and tags could be attached to their wings. The team also received permission to take blood samples from the birds to monitor their health.

Trapping condors required careful preparation and great patience. Most often, the team used a small cannon that fired a net, which opened in the air to cover the bird. However, the cannons were a fire hazard in the condors' sun-dried habitat.[9] If conditions made the risk of fire too high, the team used a pit trap, which American Indians have used for centuries. This trap consists of a camouflaged pit in which a person remains absolutely still for the many hours it may take for a bird to walk close enough to grab.

The recovery team set out fresh carcasses to bring the condors to the traps. Then they waited. Condors usually follow other scavengers

Condor R76 receives a new transmitter from biologists at Lion Canyon, California. It is only by monitoring the released condors that scientists and conservationists can tell whether their historic experiment in condor conservation is succeeding.

to a carcass and then sit on a dead tree branch or on the ground to watch—occasionally for hours. Sometimes they decide to leave without eating.

The team eventually trapped nine wild condors and fitted them with small radio transmitters. The recovery team then monitored the movements of these condors.[10]

▶ "Stealing" Eggs to Breed Condors

Stealing condor eggs to be hatched in captivity proved just as challenging as trapping the wily birds. Finding nest sites was the first challenge. Condors inspect several nest sites before choosing one, and the sites may be miles apart. Timing was essential, so the team needed to know exactly when the egg was laid. Early in the incubating stage, between the fifth day and the twenty-first day, the embryo inside the egg can be harmed by movement.

Before team members could take an egg, they had to find a level place somewhere on the rugged mountainside where a helicopter could land and whisk them and their precious cargo to a zoo. Retrieving the eggs often meant climbing down ropes to reach the nest site. Recovery team members had to be careful because condors hold their eggs on their feet. If a startled condor got up too fast, it might damage the egg. As team members

A Fish and Wildlife Service biologist crawls into the cavernous nest of a condor to remove its egg so that it can be incubated and have a better chance of hatching and developing. He replaces it with a condor egg from the San Diego Zoo.

slowly approached the nest site, they talked just loud enough that the condor would hear them. Soon the parent condor would get up carefully and walk to the entrance to investigate. Team members would then chase the parent away, take the egg, and climb to the helicopter pad.

The recovery team used a foam-insulated suitcase, which was specially made years earlier to transport whooping crane eggs, which are about the same size as condor eggs. Hot-water bottles inside the suitcase kept the egg warm, and thermometers sticking out the top measured the temperature inside.[11] By 1986 the recovery team had taken sixteen eggs for artificial incubation. Thirteen of the eggs became healthy chicks that grew up in captivity.

▶ Change of Plans

In 1984 the recovery team and conservationists compromised on a plan for the condors that would concentrate on captive breeding in the short term and on the wild population in the long term. The recovery team planned to take as many eggs and chicks as possible from the wild and keep them safe in captivity. Then, when zoos protected five young from a pair (to preserve genetic diversity), any additional young condors from that pair would be released into the wild.[12]

All plans for wild condors changed after the winter of 1984–1985. Six condors died that winter, and most of those condors were members of pairs that would lay eggs if both were still alive. In the spring of 1985, the wild population consisted of only nine birds and included only one pair.

With so few condors left, the recovery team and California Fish and Game recommended bringing all the condors left in the wild into captivity. The deaths of six condors convinced team members that leaving any birds in the wild would mean death for the remaining condors in the near future. In addition, building a captive population would be difficult without condor pairs to produce eggs. Most of the captive condors that had hatched from the stolen eggs were female. Most of the wild condors were male. Once a

Researchers fit California condors with tags and radio transmitters so that they can identify and monitor the birds after they have been released into the wild. This tagged condor perches high on a seaside cliff.

captive population was large enough to ensure that the species would not go extinct and once the condors' natural habitat could be made safe, captive condors could be released.

Condor Conservation Goes to Court

The Audubon Society, though, did not agree with these other groups and wanted some condors to be left in the wild, since it had worked to enlarge and protect the condors' natural habitat. If all condors were removed, would they be able to preserve the condors' habitat for the birds that might be released from captivity in the future? Audubon members hoped to keep the last breeding pair alive by providing clean carcasses for them to eat and monitoring them carefully. These condors could then serve as teachers to young captive condors released in the future.[13]

The disagreement between those who believed condors should be protected in captivity and those who believed the condors should be left in the wild was not a friendly one. With the preservation of the species at stake, the different groups were passionate about their own ideas of how condors should be saved, and finding a compromise seemed impossible.

The National Audubon Society took the issue to court. When the court ruled in favor of the National Audubon Society, the U.S. Fish and

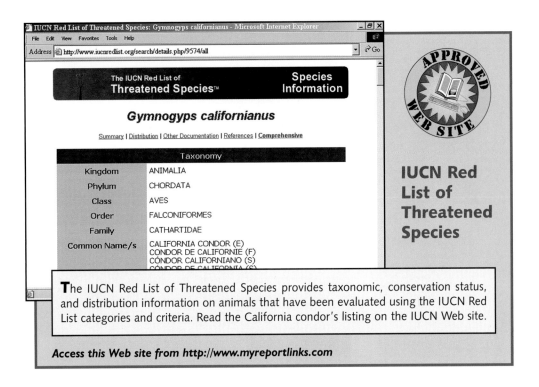

The IUCN Red List of Threatened Species provides taxonomic, conservation status, and distribution information on animals that have been evaluated using the IUCN Red List categories and criteria. Read the California condor's listing on the IUCN Web site.

Access this Web site from http://www.myreportlinks.com

Wildlife Service appealed the decision. Then in January 1986, the recovery team brought the female in the last wild pair to the San Diego Zoo's Wild Animal Park. She was very sick from lead poisoning. In spite of the best efforts of veterinarians at the zoo, the condor died. The courts then ruled in favor of the Fish and Wildlife Service, and the remaining wild condors began to be trapped.

Chapter 5

CONDORS IN CAPTIVITY

The first eggs taken from nest sites in the wild were flown by helicopter to the San Diego Zoo to be hatched in an incubator. An incubator is a sterile box that allows zookeepers to control the temperature and humidity around the egg. Zookeepers had a good idea what California condor eggs would need because researchers at the United States Geological Survey's Patuxent Wildlife Research Center in Maryland had been studying Andean condors, which are closely related to California condors.

▶ Caring for Condor Eggs

Condor eggs need to be kept warm, so the temperature in the incubators is kept between 97°F and 98°F (36°C and 36.7°C). The amount of humidity, or moisture in the air, around the eggs is also important. During the long incubation, eggs gradually lose moisture through pores in the eggshell. If the air around an egg is too dry, and the egg loses too much moisture, the chick may become dehydrated, not grow large enough, and be too weak to hatch. If the air is too humid, not enough moisture evaporates, which causes the chick to be swollen with water. A swollen chick may be too big to turn in the egg to get in the right position for hatching.[1] Zookeepers weigh the eggs each day to be sure they are losing moisture at the right rate. Condor eggs should lose about 12 to 14 percent of their initial weight during incubation.[2]

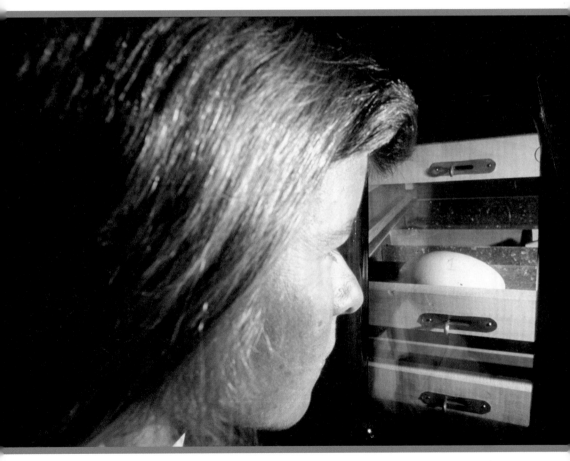

A researcher from the San Diego Zoo checks on the condition of a California condor egg in one of the zoo's incubators. Under controlled conditions, with no threat from predators, incubated condor eggs have a much greater survival rate than condor eggs in the wild.

The eggs also need to be kept free of bacteria, which can enter the egg through the pores and kill the embryo. (While it is inside the egg, the chick is an embryo.) Whenever people handle an egg, they use sterile gloves, and everything that touches the egg is sterile.

In the wild, conditions are neither sterile nor constant for a condor egg. The condor parents keep the egg warm in the feathers of their chest, but both parents may leave the egg at times and allow it to cool. Sometimes, parents fight over which one will sit on the egg. As they fight, they may leave the egg uncovered or accidentally kick it. The care that condor eggs receive in incubators results in a higher percentage of healthy chicks. Only 40 to 50 percent of eggs incubated in the wild produce chicks that live long enough to learn to fly. Between 1983 and 1986, the survival rate for the incubated eggs was 81 percent.[3]

▶From Egg to Chick

About the fifth day after the egg is laid, the embryo begins to form blood vessels connecting it to the membrane inside the eggshell. As the embryo grows, it receives nourishment from the yolk. At the large end of the egg is a pouch of air that forms as the moisture in the egg evaporates.

About a week before the embryo will hatch, it breaks into this air pouch and breathes air for the first time. Keepers can tell when this happens, and they move the egg into a hatching incubator.[4]

At the San Diego Zoo, zookeepers check on eggs every hour during the hatching process. Every odd-numbered hour, they play a recording of condor noises and tap lightly on the egg. On even-numbered hours, they check to see what the chick is doing. It may be moving in the egg or nibbling at it.[5]

The air pouch contains only enough air for a day or two. The embryo must make a hole in the egg, called a pip, so that it can breathe air outside the egg. It makes the hole with a sharp bump on its beak, called the egg tooth, which disappears after it

This San Diego Zoo Web site offers an overview of the California condor. Read about some of the historical milestones in California condor conservation and find additional information about the captive breeding and reintroduction of this endangered bird.

Access this Web site from http://www.myreportlinks.com

hatches. When keepers see the pip, they adjust the humidity around the egg, adding moisture to prevent membranes inside the egg from drying out.

During the next few days, the chick absorbs the yolk into its stomach. Gradually the blood vessels connected to the egg membranes dry up. Then the chick is ready to hatch. After making the air hole bigger, it turns slowly inside the shell and uses its egg tooth to break a line around the shell. Condor eggshells are thick, much thicker than the shell of a chicken egg. Sometimes the condor chick needs help breaking out of an egg.

Assisted Hatching

Before the first condor eggs were taken from the wild, observers had seen condor parents nibble at the hole made by their chick to help it hatch. Zookeepers at the San Diego Zoo practiced assisted hatching on chicken eggs so they would be ready to help the first condor chicks hatch in captivity. The procedure needs to be done very carefully because some blood may still be circulating in blood vessels attached to the membrane. If a piece of shell attached to one of these vessels is broken away, the chick could bleed to death.[6]

Caring for Chicks

A few hours after the chick hatches, zookeepers move it to a brooder box where it can be kept warm. Standing behind a dark curtain, a zookeeper reaches an arm into the box to give the chick its first meal of ground mice and water. The zookeeper's arm, however, is disguised. People caring for condor chicks use puppets designed to look like the head of an adult condor to feed and care for the chick. The puppet helps the chick know that it is a condor. If it saw people right away, it might think it was supposed to be a person.

At first, chicks are fed every couple of hours. Within a few days, they can pick up food from a small bowl. The chicks grow fast. They weigh about seven ounces (nearly two hundred grams) when they hatch. Three weeks later, they weigh two and a half pounds (slightly more than one kilogram).[7]

The first condor chick to hatch in captivity was named Sisquoc, an American Indian name. (All captive condors are given American Indian names.)

▶ Puppet Parents

At first, all of the incubated eggs were raised by keepers wearing condor puppets. Zookeepers used the puppets to help chicks develop socially. The puppet "beaks" cleaned the chicks' downy feathers, and the zookeepers used the puppets to play with chicks the way that condor parents would have. The puppets were also made to look alert in response to strange sounds to teach chicks to be

Oregon Zoo Conservation - Microsoft Internet Explorer

File   Edit   View   Favorites   Tools   Help

Address http://www.oregonzoo.org/Condors/tatoosh.htm

Tatoosh took her first drink of water from the pool during the afternoon heatwave. Both foster parents spent a great amount of time on the ground showing little Tatoosh how to get around

Tatoosh, a three-and-a-half-month-old chick born at the Oregon Zoo, is one of the featured subjects of **Oregon Zoo's California Condors**. In 2003, the zoo became the fourth California condor breeding facility in the United States.

EDITOR'S CHOICE

aware of their environment. In trying to prevent chicks from ever seeing them, zookeepers communicated silently with written notes and gestures and used recorded sounds from outdoors to mimic the birds' natural environment.

In the early years of captive breeding, the zookeepers' priority was to increase the number of condors. They quickly took eggs from condor parents and hatched the eggs in the safety of incubators. In this way, they encouraged the parents to lay another egg.

More recently, zookeepers have been moving condor eggs from parents to incubators and back to parents. Sometimes, zookeepers take the egg to the safety of an incubator and give the parents a dummy egg to incubate. When the real egg is about to hatch, the keepers switch it with the dummy egg.

Adult Condors in Captivity

When the last wild condor arrived at the San Diego Zoo in April 1987, twenty-seven condors lived in captivity; fourteen condors lived at the San Diego Wild Animal Park and thirteen at the Los Angeles Zoo. Seventeen of the captive condors had been raised in captivity.

The San Diego Zoo houses condors in six enclosures in its "condor-minium." Each enclosure has approximately 3,200 square feet (297 square meters) of ground space and a 22-foot (6.7-meter) mesh ceiling to allow condors to exercise their wings. The enclosures include pools and roosting and nesting areas.[8]

The zoos keep condors at a distance from areas that are open to the public. Condors have been on display at the World Center for Wild Birds of Prey in Boise, Idaho, since 1997. In 2000, San Diego's Wild Animal Park opened its Condor Ridge where people can see condors that are not in the breeding program.

▲ The world must seem upside down for the reintroduced California condor, with its eggs being stolen and replaced, its chicks being fed by puppets, and its food still being supplied by humans. All these measures to save the species are intended to be temporary, but for how long?

In captivity, condors eat rabbits, rats, trout, and a specially prepared ground meat. Zookeepers vary the diet, and they do not feed condors every day, since they would not eat that often in the wild.

▶Preserving Condor Genes

The zoos needed to do more than make the condors comfortable. Their goal was to bring many more condors into the world and then release the birds into the wild again. However, condors had never produced young in captivity, and no one knew if they would. Condors need to bond and become a pair before they will produce an egg. At first, scientists did not really know how condors chose mates, so they could not be sure that putting a male and a female together would result in a mated pair.

Zookeepers had another worry, and that had to do with genetics, the study of genes. Genes are molecules that parents pass on to their offspring, making them resemble others of their kind. Genes determine the kinds of proteins a bird, for example, produces, and the proteins, in turn, determine what the bird will look like and how it will act.

A gene pool is the total number of genes in a species. Each individual in the species will have some of the genes in the gene pool but not all of them. When the species is doing well, the gene pool contains a wide variety of genes, including many that may not have any particular use. Over time, a species' gene pool changes. Gradually, harmful genes—such as genes that cause an individual to get sick often—tend to disappear. Other genes change, or mutate, and these mutated genes help the species adapt to changes in its environment.

However, when a species contains only a few individuals, the gene pool becomes smaller. Harmful genes last longer, and fewer genes mutate to adapt to new conditions. In a small population, many of the individuals may be related. When related individuals mate and reproduce, the genes they pass on to the next generation are similar. If all the individuals in a

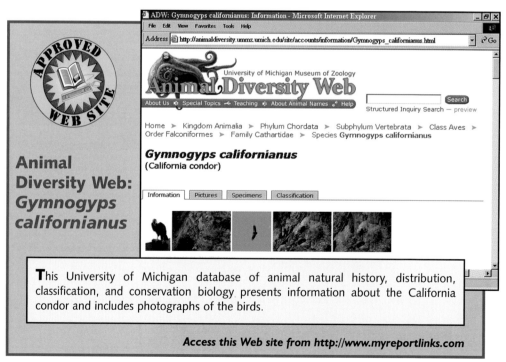

Animal Diversity Web: *Gymnogyps californianus*

This University of Michigan database of animal natural history, distribution, classification, and conservation biology presents information about the California condor and includes photographs of the birds.

Access this Web site from http://www.myreportlinks.com

species have similar genes, they are all susceptible to the same diseases and less able to adapt to change.

The idea that zookeepers should know which genes each individual carried before putting males and females together was still new in the 1980s. However, the Zoological Society of San Diego opened its Center for Reproduction of Endangered Species, which put together the world's largest team of zoo-based researchers to study the genes of endangered species. The center, now known as the center for Conservation and Research for Endangered Species, or CRES, was able to identify condors' genes and use what they learned to decide which condors to pair.

When they examined blood samples, scientists determined that the captive condors were all rather closely related.[9] The scientists also noted that some were more closely related than others, and they identified three clans, or family lines. The scientists used this information to try to preserve as much of the remaining gene pool as possible.

Lessons in Condor Social Behavior

The question remained whether condors would bond and reproduce in captivity. In the wild, condors choose their own mates. How would they react to mates chosen for them?

Zookeepers soon learned that condor society is hierarchical, which means that each bird has a place in the society. The individual's place has a higher or lower rank relative to other birds. Condors prefer mates with a similar social rank. At the same time, males should be dominant in the pair.

These social aspects of pair bonding resulted in some trial and error as zookeepers put condors together. For example, one of the females taken from the wild in 1986 proved to have a high social

▲ The majestic wingspan of an adult California condor is a wondrous thing to behold.

rank and a dominant personality. Zookeepers put her with several potential mates before finding one with a strong enough personality to be accepted.

In spite of some difficulties, most of the condors bonded with chosen mates. Then in 1988, a condor at the San Diego Zoo laid an egg. The event was important because it showed that the condors would bond and mate in captivity. However, captive condors at the National Zoo had laid eggs early in the 1900s, but none of the eggs was fertile and no chicks hatched. Everyone involved with the condors waited anxiously until zookeepers could be sure that the egg could become a chick.

Molloko

Even before the condor mother laid the egg, zookeepers were watching her intently through a closed-circuit monitor. As soon as they saw the egg, they took it, checked it for cracks, and measured it. Then they kept it warm in an incubator and checked it each day for evidence that it would produce a chick.

When scientists learned that the egg was fertile, everyone involved in condor conservation breathed a sigh of relief. Until that moment, no one could be sure that condors would produce chicks in captivity. If they did not, the species was

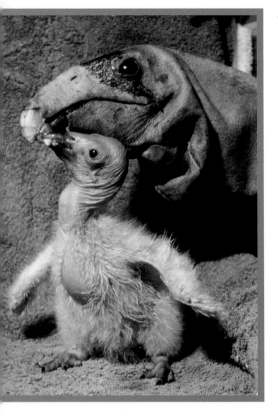

Hoy, a California condor chick, is the second generation of his family to be born in captivity. His mother, Molloko, was also born at the San Diego Zoo. Here, Hoy is being fed by a condor puppet on the arm of a zookeeper. People working to save condors try to disguise themselves so that the birds will not imprint on them—become attached to them or become less wild than they will need to be when they are finally released.

doomed to extinction. The chick hatched on April 29, 1988, and was named Molloko.[10] She was the only condor to hatch that year. In 1989, three more chicks hatched at the San Diego Zoo and one hatched at the Los Angeles Zoo.

By 1993, seventy-one condors lived at the Los Angeles Zoo and the San Diego Wild Animal Park. Because both facilities were full, twelve birds were sent to the Peregrine Fund's World Center for Birds of Prey in Boise, Idaho. The numbers continued to increase, even as condors were released into the wild. In 2003, the Oregon Zoo also began a captive-breeding program with twelve birds.

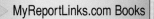
Chapter 6 ▶

FREE AGAIN

From the beginning, the captive-breeding program was intended to keep California condors captive only to save the species and then release the birds into the mountains where they had once lived. The goal was to have wild California condors again. However, the California Condor Recovery Team had questions to answer and problems to solve before the release of captive condors could begin.

▷ Preserving Habitat

One problem was that some people thought there was no reason to preserve condor habitat once there were no condors left in the wild. Mining and other activities were not allowed in some areas set aside for condors. With no condors to disturb, people saw no reason not to use the land.

Conservationists with the Audubon Society, the Wilderness Society, and other groups had worked hard to provide habitat for the condors. During the time all wild condors were being protected in captivity, these conservation groups continued to watch over the habitat that condors would return

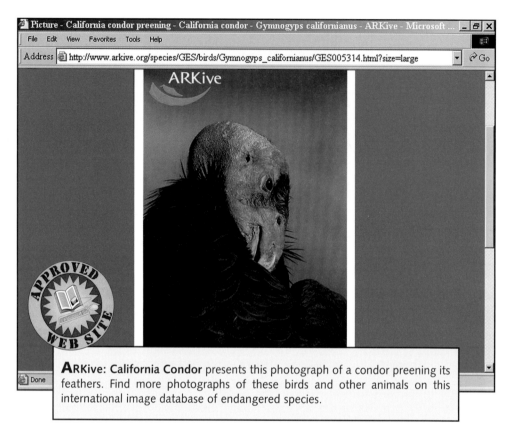

ARKive: California Condor presents this photograph of a condor preening its feathers. Find more photographs of these birds and other animals on this international image database of endangered species.

to. Conservationists paid attention to revised regulations that might affect condor habitat and kept in touch with California lawmakers.

▶Preserving Genes

Another problem was the species' gene pool. To be healthy in the long term, a species needs variety in its gene pool. When all the living condors were in captivity, scientists realized that all future condors would be descended from only fourteen "founder" parents. These condors were called founders because they would be the foundation of the future condor species.

Scientists wanted to be sure that they could preserve as much of the gene pool as possible. At first the California Condor Recovery Team decided that at least five chicks from each of the original pairs should be kept in captivity to preserve genetic variety. However, some founders died before producing five captive offspring. At the same time, an analysis of each condor's genes allowed scientists to develop a pedigree for each condor. Chicks could be chosen for release if other captive condors had similar genetic pedigrees.[1]

Survival in the Wild

A third question was whether condors born in a zoo could survive in the wild. Because all the birds had been captured, there were no wild condors to teach released birds how to survive. Could young condors learn to survive on their own?

To answer this question, the recovery team decided to release young Andean condors into California condor habitat. Biologists at the Patuxent Wildlife Research Center had been raising the South American condors and studying their biology and behavior. The Andean condors are closely related to California condors but are not as endangered. Scientists thought they could risk the lives of a few Andean condors to get a better idea of how well California condors would adjust to life in the wild. Andean condors, they thought, would behave the way California condors would. By watching the Andean condors, the recovery team could learn more about ways to care for released birds and practice tracking their movements.

The Andean condors would serve another purpose. Their presence would remind people that condor habitat should still be protected.

Andean Condors in California

In 1988, seven young Andean condors arrived at release sites in California. Three were taken to the Hopper Mountain National Wildlife Refuge, and four were taken to the Sespe Condor Sanctuary. The young birds lived in roost boxes that opened to large pens with netting that allowed them to see their surroundings. When they were about eight months old and had learned to fly, the netting was removed. The following year, six more Andean condors arrived at the release pen.

After the Andean condors were allowed to fly free, the recovery team provided carcasses for them. Biologists were happy to see the condors feeding on these carcasses regularly.[2] As long as the birds ate meals provided by the recovery team, they were less likely to swallow lead fragments in carcasses left by hunters.

Generally the Andean condors did well in California condor habitat. One died when she flew into a power line, and the recovery team noticed

Color Photo of the California Condor (Gymnogyps californianus) - Microsoft Internet Explorer

File   Edit   View   Favorites   Tools   Help

Address http://www.ecology.info/condors-fig-1.htm

about
students
teachers
instructions
 for authors
donate photos
 and artwork
translate
copyright
disclaimer
faqs
write us
home

bahasa melayu
castellano

California Condor (*Gymnogyps californianus*)
and Canyon National Park, Arizona, USA. Note the
dist

A California condor sails above the Grand Canyon in this photograph from the **Ecology of Condors** Web site. The site, which features ecological information written by experts in the field, includes facts about both the California condor and Andean condor, found only in the Western Hemisphere.

that the Andean condors often visited areas where people lived.

Based on their observations of the Andean condors in the wild, the California Condor Recovery Team decided it was time to release California condors. By removing eggs so that condor parents would produce additional eggs, zookeepers had almost doubled the number of living condors. In 1986, when the recovery team began capturing all wild condors, no one could be certain the condors would breed in captivity. The biologists considered the possibility that the species would soon be extinct. Five years later, more than fifty condors lived at the captive-breeding sites.[3] By the end of 1993, all of the Andean condors that had been released in California were captured and released again in South America.

California Condors in the Wild Again

Two California condors, a male named Chocuyens and a female named Xewe, were released in the

▲ An Andean condor, native to South America, is the only other condor found in the Western Hemisphere. The California Condor Recovery Team used Andean condors to determine when it might be time to finally try releasing California condors in the wild.

Sespe sanctuary in January 1992. Chocuyens and Xewe hatched in 1991 and were chosen for release because each had five siblings in captivity and because keepers thought they would do well in the wild. They were the only California condors that met all the criteria for release. To make the release group larger, the recovery team put two more Andean condors in the release pen with them.

The recovery team put small transmitters on the two California condors, one transmitter on each wing. They also attached large red-and-white tags with numbers to make the condors easier to identify.

For a while, the two California condors seemed to do well. Then, in October, Chocuyens died after drinking from a puddle of antifreeze drained from someone's car. That left Xewe alone in the wild.

Second Release

In December 1992, six California condors arrived at the release pen in the Sespe Condor Sanctuary. These young condors, born earlier that year, had been raised as a group. Zookeepers hoped that raising condor chicks together would help them bond and learn to be condors.

In the wild, condors lay only one egg, so condor chicks do not get to know other condors until they learn to fly. The young condors in the release pen in 1992 never knew real condor parents. They were raised by humans wearing hand puppets.

The condors did bond, but without parents to teach them how to behave, the birds did not know enough to stay out of trouble. To the researchers, it appeared that the young condors were behaving like a teenage "gang."[4] Since the recovery team provided food for them, they did not have to spend hours searching for it. Instead of flying off

▲ Condor 10 perches on the edge of a cliff in the Grand Canyon. A radio transmitter helps members of the recovery team monitor the bird.

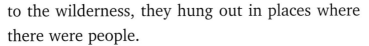

to the wilderness, they hung out in places where there were people.

Places where people live often include power lines, and the condors seemed attracted to utility poles. To them, the poles looked like perfect roosting places. However, three young condors died after colliding with power lines.

Acting Tame in the Wild

Hoping to get the condors away from people, the recovery team built another release site in a more remote area of Los Padres National Forest and brought five young captive condors to this new site. The biologists also captured the four condors still living in the Sespe sanctuary, including Xewe, and brought them to the new release site.

The condors continued to act tame. One resident of the Pine Mountain Club, a mountain community, reported finding young condors in his second-floor bedroom, ripping his mattress apart. They had landed on the deck outside the bedroom and had made a hole in the screen door.[5] One condor walked into an office building to look around.[6]

In 1994, biologists captured the older condors and returned them to captivity. Then one of the young condors in the most recent release group died after flying into power lines. Biologists realized they would need to teach the captive condors to be afraid of power lines and people—in other words, teach them to be truly wild.

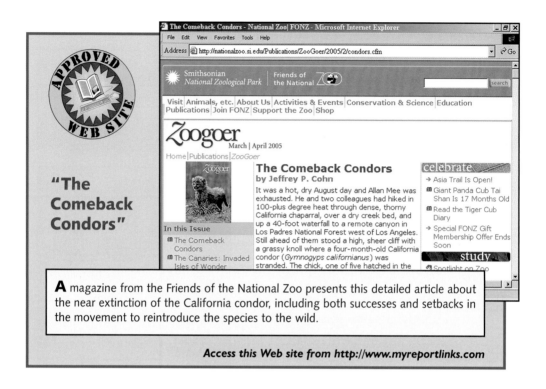

"The Comeback Condors"

The Comeback Condors - National Zoo| FONZ - Microsoft Internet Explorer

File   Edit   View   Favorites   Tools   Help

Address http://nationalzoo.si.edu/Publications/ZooGoer/2005/2/condors.cfm   Go

Smithsonian *National Zoological Park* | Friends of the National

Visit | Animals, etc. | About Us | Activities & Events | Conservation & Science | Education
Publications | Join FONZ | Support the Zoo | Shop

Zoogoer   March | April 2005

Home | Publications | *ZooGoer*

In this Issue
- The Comeback Condors
- The Canaries: Invaded Isles of Wonder

The Comeback Condors
by Jeffrey P. Cohn

It was a hot, dry August day and Allan Mee was exhausted. He and two colleagues had hiked in 100-plus degree heat through dense, thorny California chaparral, over a dry creek bed, and up a 40-foot waterfall to a remote canyon in Los Padres National Forest west of Los Angeles. Still ahead of them stood a high, sheer cliff with a grassy knoll where a four-month-old California condor (*Gymnogyps californianus*) was stranded. The chick, one of five hatched in the

celebrate
→ Asia Trail Is Open!
- Giant Panda Cub Tai Shan Is 17 Months Old
- Read the Tiger Cub Diary
→ Special FONZ Gift Membership Offer Ends Soon

study
- Spotlight on Zoo

A magazine from the Friends of the National Zoo presents this detailed article about the near extinction of the California condor, including both successes and setbacks in the movement to reintroduce the species to the wild.

Access this Web site from http://www.myreportlinks.com

Aversion Training

When the next group of young condors arrived at the release site in 1995, there was something new in the pen. It looked like a pole for high voltage wires—something the young condors had never seen before. The fake pole was wired so that a condor landing on it would get a shock. The condors learned quickly to avoid the pole. In fact, some condors learned by watching other condors react to the shock.[7]

In addition, keepers at zoos began to teach young condors that people should be avoided. The keepers ran at the condors, waving their arms and shouting. They captured condors and shoved them in kennels. Harassing the condors was part of aversion training to teach condors to stay away from people.

The aversion training brought good results. The condors released in 1995 did stay away from poles with high voltage wires. They did not stay away from people, though. Condors still landed on rooftops and flew into campsites.

▶ Problems With Puppet-Raised Condors

Between 1992 and 1996, all of the young condors released in California were hatched in incubators and raised by people wearing condor puppets. Some biologists feel certain that the puppets never

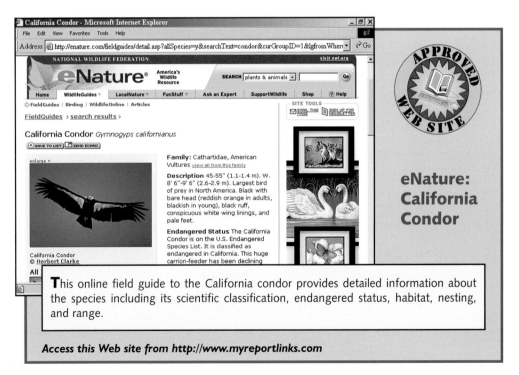

eNature: California Condor

This online field guide to the California condor provides detailed information about the species including its scientific classification, endangered status, habitat, nesting, and range.

Access this Web site from http://www.myreportlinks.com

fooled the chicks for long; the young birds knew people were feeding them. The chicks might be seeing a puppet, but they could probably hear sounds made by people and machines. Sometimes the curious chicks poked their heads into the hole the puppet parent came through and could see the person holding the puppet.[8]

Later as the number of condors increased rapidly, some condor parents were allowed to raise their own chicks, and zookeepers had opportunities to watch what those parents did. The keepers noticed that condor parents are not as gentle as the puppets were. Sometimes, condor parents peck at their chicks or push them away when they get too curious. They seem to be teaching their chicks to be cautious and wary. Perhaps the puppet parents were not teaching condor chicks what they needed to know to be wild.

▶ Frustration, Then Success

In the meantime, biologists whose job it was to monitor the released condors felt frustrated by the birds' behavior. Some believed that condors raised by puppets would always be too tame to do well in the wild. All of the condors released in 1992 and 1993 either died or were captured and returned to captivity.[9] The fourteen condors released in 1995 remained in the wild. Their aversion training taught them to stay away from power

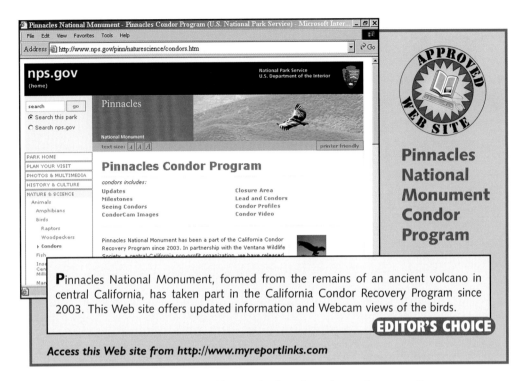

lines, but they still needed to be chased away from residential areas.

In 1996 the recovery team released four young condors that had spent the first three months of their lives with their parents. Just a few months with condor parents seemed to make these young condors more like wild condors and better able to adjust to life in the wild.

▶ A Second Condor Population

As field biologists worked to monitor the young condors released in California, the recovery team finalized plans to release condors in Arizona. The California Condor Recovery Plan called for three separate condor populations: one in captivity and two in the wild. The wild populations were to be many miles apart. Separate wild populations increase chances for the species' survival because there is always the chance that a population in one area might be destroyed by disease or a natural disaster such as an earthquake.

By 1991 the team had selected an area in northern Arizona to release condors. Scientists determined that condors had lived in this area about ten thousand years ago, and the region still provided a large area of remote countryside with cliffs and caves. The process of evaluating the release site in Arizona was long and complicated, involving twenty-five criteria divided into three levels by priority.[10] Finally the team decided on the Vermilion Cliffs area, about fifty miles northwest of the Grand Canyon.

Persuading the Public

Before the team could release condors at Vermilion Cliffs, team members needed to persuade the public to accept the plan. This process took several years, not because people did not want condors, but because they did not want the government to interfere with their lives.[11] Federal protection of endangered species puts restrictions on activities within the endangered species' critical habitat. Someone who owns land in an area determined to be critical habitat may not be able to sell that land, and a hunter who accidentally shoots a condor might go to jail.

Experimental and Nonessential

To make the presence of condors less threatening to people, the U.S. Fish and Wildlife Service decided the Arizona condors would be considered an experimental, nonessential population. Because the Arizona condors would be the second wild

▲ *California condors find a rocky ledge of the Grand Canyon to perch on.*

population, distant from the first, the population qualified as experimental. An experimental population is treated as if it belongs to a threatened species rather than an endangered one.

The U.S. Fish and Wildlife Service also decided that the second population could be considered nonessential because captive breeding had been so successful. Loss of the Arizona population would not threaten the survival of the species. A nonessential population receives only a few of the protections provided by the Endangered Species Act. For example, a hunter who accidentally kills an Arizona condor while following safe hunting procedures will not be prosecuted.

The recovery team also found a partner, the Peregrine Fund, to manage the Arizona condors and help fund the project. The Peregrine Fund had successfully established self-sustaining populations of birds of prey, including the peregrine falcon, in the past.

▶ Condors Arrive in Arizona

In 1996, six parent-raised young California condors arrived at the Vermilion Cliffs area in Arizona. After one of the first condors released in Arizona died from a collision with power lines, all condors released at Vermilion Cliffs also received aversion training to teach them to stay away from poles holding power lines. The California condors

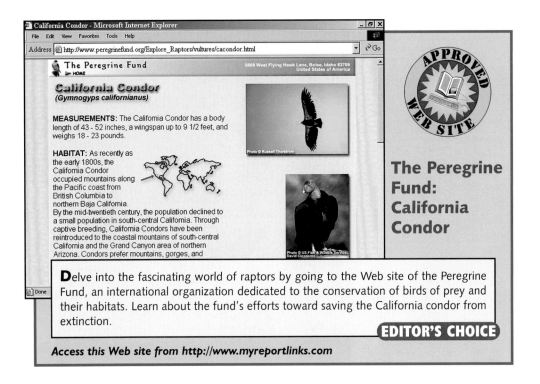

California Condor - Microsoft Internet Explorer

File   Edit   View   Favorites   Tools   Help

Address http://www.peregrinefund.org/Explore_Raptors/vultures/cacondor.html   Go

The Peregrine Fund
HOME
5668 West Flying Hawk Lane, Boise, Idaho 83709
United States of America

California Condor
(Gymnogyps californianus)

MEASUREMENTS: The California Condor has a body length of 43 - 52 inches, a wingspan up to 9 1/2 feet, and weighs 18 - 23 pounds.

HABITAT: As recently as the early 1800s, the California Condor occupied mountains along the Pacific coast from British Columbia to northern Baja California. By the mid-twentieth century, the population declined to a small population in south-central California. Through captive breeding, California Condors have been reintroduced to the coastal mountains of south-central California and the Grand Canyon area of northern Arizona. Condors prefer mountains, gorges, and

Photo © Russell Thorstrom

Photo © US Fish & Wildlife Service, David Clendenen

The Peregrine Fund: California Condor

Delve into the fascinating world of raptors by going to the Web site of the Peregrine Fund, an international organization dedicated to the conservation of birds of prey and their habitats. Learn about the fund's efforts toward saving the California condor from extinction.

EDITOR'S CHOICE

Access this Web site from http://www.myreportlinks.com

in Arizona also wore radio transmitters and large tags with numbers. Unfortunately, like the young condors in southern California, the condors released in Arizona soon got into trouble.

Some of the young condors were so curious about people that they went close enough to pull at shoelaces.[12] They visited Grand Canyon visitor centers, and destroyed one camper's campsite.

The Peregrine Fund field biologists, like the field biologists in California, chased condors away from buildings and places where people gathered. But they decided to give the young condors a chance to grow up rather than returning them to captivity right away. Some of the most assertive

Condor Released in Arizona - Raptor Center at the University of Minnesota - Microsoft Internet Explorer

File Edit View Favorites Tools Help

Address http://www.raptor.cvm.umn.edu/raptor/news/Condorreleased.html Go

UNIVERSITY OF MINNESOTA   One Stop | Directories | Search U of M

The Raptor Center   Veterinary Medicine

What's Inside

About the Raptor Center

Educational Programs

Make a Donation

Volunteer Opportunities

News and Events

Recycling for Raptors

Contact The Raptor Center

Directions and Map

Home > News and Events > Condor Released in Arizona

Condor Released in Arizona   PRINT   MAIL

Raptor Center at the University of Minnesota, a Web page of the University of Minnesota, College of Veterinary Medicine, offers this photograph of a young California condor making its return to the wild from this pinnacle near the Vermilion Cliffs National Monument in Arizona. The Raptor Center's vets treated the condor for a broken wing.

and least cautious birds found themselves back in captivity for a few days or a few weeks in "detention." But most of them were returned to the wild.

Condors in Big Sur

Meanwhile, the recovery team continued to release condors in California. In 1997, the recovery team took young California condors to the Ventana Wilderness area in central California, which includes the northern Santa Lucia Mountains and Big Sur coast. Condors had not been seen there since the early 1900s.

Chapter 7

NOT YET WILD

As long as the California condor recovery program has existed, dedicated field biologists and zoo-keepers have worked long hours protecting the condors, feeding them, and caring for them when they are sick. These people experience a great loss when a condor dies, and they feel frustrated when a condor does not adjust to the wild. They have not given up, though, and continue to try new ideas. Recently, the people involved in condor conservation have had reason to celebrate.

▶ Mentors

One new idea that has proven successful is the use of mature mentor condors to help young condors in captivity learn how to be condors. Biologists put a mature condor with young condors for several months before the young condors are released. They found that the young condors that lived with a mentor before their release were less likely to come close to people and were better at fitting into condor society. Usually the

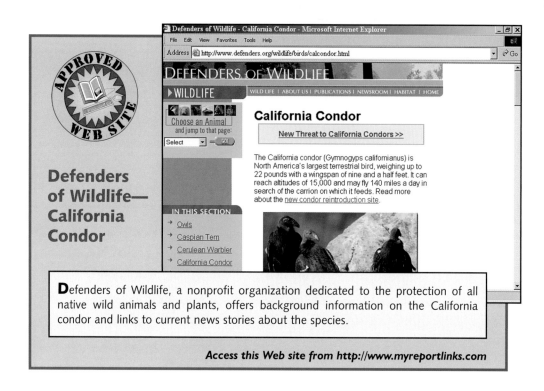

Defenders of Wildlife— California Condor

Defenders of Wildlife - California Condor - Microsoft Internet Explorer

File Edit View Favorites Tools Help

Address http://www.defenders.org/wildlife/birds/calcondor.html Go

DEFENDERS OF WILDLIFE

▶WILDLIFE WILD LIFE | ABOUT US | PUBLICATIONS | NEWSROOM | HABITAT | HOME

Choose an Animal
and jump to that page:
Select

California Condor

New Threat to California Condors >>

The California condor (Gymnogyps californianus) is North America's largest terrestrial bird, weighing up to 22 pounds with a wingspan of nine and a half feet. It can reach altitudes of 15,000 and may fly 140 miles a day in search of the carrion on which it feeds. Read more about the new condor reintroduction site.

IN THIS SECTION

→ Owls
→ Caspian Tern
→ Cerulean Warbler
→ California Condor

Defenders of Wildlife, a nonprofit organization dedicated to the protection of all native wild animals and plants, offers background information on the California condor and links to current news stories about the species.

Access this Web site from http://www.myreportlinks.com

mentor condor lives in the release pen with the younger condors but is not released with them.

A mentor condor that was released was AC-8 (Adult Condor Number Eight), also known as the matriarch because she provided so many eggs. In 2000 she returned to the Sespe wilderness area that had been her home for about twenty-five years before she was captured in 1986. Team members hoped she would teach the puppet-raised young condors how to be wild. At first she chased young condors away, but she soon began to fly with them and show them her routes to foraging areas and her favorite perches.[1]

To the great sorrow of all involved in the birds' recovery, a poacher shot and killed AC-8 in 2003. Investigators used the rifle shell to discover who the shooter was. Since California condors are a federally protected species, shooting them is a crime that can result in a jail sentence. In this case, prosecutors believed Britton Cole Lewis when he claimed he did not know he was shooting a condor and gave him a lighter sentence. He was fined $20,000, had to forfeit his firearm, and was required to do two hundred hours of community service.[2]

Condor Social Behavior

Biologists continue to find evidence that condors are more social than anyone had expected. Condors often roost together and follow one another to foraging areas. Apparently, condors sometimes choose to get together just to hang out. As condors released in the Big Sur area expanded their range, some discovered another group of condors released in Ventura County, more than 150 miles south. Since then, Big Sur condors have occasionally flown the long distance to visit their southern cousins.[3]

The complex social rules in condor society can work against them, though. For example, biologists realized that a high-ranking female will choose to have no mate at all rather than one of lower social rank.[4]

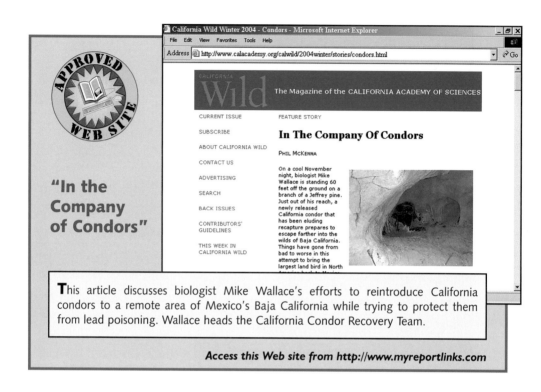

"In the Company of Condors"

California Wild Winter 2004 - Condors - Microsoft Internet Explorer

File   Edit   View   Favorites   Tools   Help

Address http://www.calacademy.org/calwild/2004winter/stories/condors.html   Go

CALIFORNIA

Wild   The Magazine of the CALIFORNIA ACADEMY OF SCIENCES

CURRENT ISSUE

SUBSCRIBE

ABOUT CALIFORNIA WILD

CONTACT US

ADVERTISING

SEARCH

BACK ISSUES

CONTRIBUTORS' GUIDELINES

THIS WEEK IN CALIFORNIA WILD

FEATURE STORY

In The Company Of Condors

PHIL MCKENNA

On a cool November night, biologist Mike Wallace is standing 60 feet off the ground on a branch of a Jeffrey pine. Just out of his reach, a newly released California condor that has been eluding recapture prepares to escape farther into the wilds of Baja California. Things have gone from bad to worse in this attempt to bring the largest land bird in North

This article discusses biologist Mike Wallace's efforts to reintroduce California condors to a remote area of Mexico's Baja California while trying to protect them from lead poisoning. Wallace heads the California Condor Recovery Team.

Access this Web site from http://www.myreportlinks.com

▷ Milestones

After years of tracking young condors and chasing the curious young birds away from homes and visitor centers, recovery team members began to see the misbehaving puppet-raised condors grow up and form pairs. In 2001, an Arizona condor laid the first egg to be laid in the wild in fifteen years. That egg was later found broken, but a chick did hatch in the wild the following year.

Another milestone had come in 1999 when two condors fed on a dead sea lion along the Big Sur coast.[5] Biologists were pleased to see that the condors were able to find food for themselves.

They were even more pleased that the food was a sea lion.

Several hundred years ago, mammals that live in the ocean, including sea lions, seals, and whales, probably provided an important source of food for the condors. Beginning in the 1700s, condors switched to land animals because the sudden abundance of cattle in California resulted in a good supply of carcasses. At the same time, large-scale hunting of whales and seals caused that food supply to become scarce.

Recently, sea lion and seal populations have increased along the Pacific coast. It is hoped that this new food supply will help condors expand their range along the West coast. To help condors

This news article examines a proposal by Stanford researchers to release captive-bred condors near seal and sea lion breeding groups on the West coast. By feasting on the carrion of these marine mammals, the condors will be eating the same diet their ancestors did.

Access this Web site from http://www.myreportlinks.com

learn to eat sea lion carcasses, conservationists have set up a release site near the sea lions.[6]

Lead Poisoning Remains a Threat

Recovery team members were glad to see young condors expand their range and behave like wild condors. Part of wild condor behavior, though, is finding food. As wild condors became wilder, they began to feed on carcasses left by hunters. In those carcasses were bullet fragments, containing lead, which the condors swallowed.

Biologists monitoring the Arizona condors saw no evidence of lead poisoning in the first four years of the program. Then in 2000, three condors died from lead poisoning. A fourth disappeared and may also have died from lead poisoning. Tests on the other Arizona condors showed that ten of them required treatment for high levels of lead in their blood.[7]

The treatment for lead poisoning in condors is called chelation, and it requires capturing the condors and injecting a calcium formula twice a day. The procedure is painful and stressful for the captured birds, and the long-term side effects of the treatment are not known.

By December 2002, another Arizona condor was found dead from lead poisoning. Between 1996 and 2002, condors were treated for high levels of lead in their blood twenty-four times.[8]

A pair of reintroduced condors, raised in captivity, now make their home in the wild at Castle Crags, California.

Biologists take blood samples from condors from all release sites regularly. Periodically they bring condors back to zoos to remove lead fragments surgically or treat sick condors with chelation.

Solutions and Signs of Hope

Conservationists and others concerned with our environment are taking steps to make condor habitat safer for the birds. Public education campaigns encourage hunters to bury gut piles (what is left after hunters skin and clean animals they have killed) so that condors will not find them.[9]

Hunters are also being encouraged to use bullets and shot made from materials other than lead. Recently, nontoxic bullets that work as well as lead bullets have become available to hunters. By educating hunters about the dangers that lead ammunition poses to condors and other scavenging wildlife, lead poisoning could become a thing of the past.

In 2006 a California assemblyman introduced a bill that would require hunters to use lead-free ammunition in condor country. Unfortunately, the bill did not move beyond the California legislature's Water, Parks and Wildlife Committee.[10]

A year later, however, the Tejon Ranch Company, owners of the state's largest privately owned parcel of land, which allows hunting on some of its grounds, announced a ban on all lead ammunition by its hunters. The ranch is also an area that has been used for years by California condors to forage and roost. The ban, which will go into effect in 2008, is the first by a large private wildlife management group in California. Hailed by conservation groups, it shows that private landowners can make a difference in saving endangered species like the California condor.[11]

Other Environmental Hazards

Lead is not the only material used by humans that is causing problems for California condors. Three chicks that died after hatching in the wild were taken to the San Diego Zoo's department of Conservation and Research for Endangered Species. Biologists there found that two of the chicks had swallowed a variety of trash, from bottle caps to glass.[12]

Biologists think some of the trash may have been in the nest site, brought there by ravens. Condor parents may have deliberately fed small, hard fragments to their young, mistaking the trash for bone fragments, which provide calcium for their chicks.

A Measure of Success

California condors are flying freely today, but they are not really wild—and they are not out of danger. Each year, more young condors are released into the wild, and each year, pairs of condors produce eggs in the wild. Field biologists watch the young condors carefully. They also monitor previously released condors, which all have little transmitters on their wings. The field biologists trap condors regularly to take blood samples and take condors in for treatment when necessary.

This degree of care has saved many condors from death. One wild-hatched chick broke its wing and was taken to San Diego so the broken bone could be set. Other young condors are returned to captivity if they lose weight after release or show other signs of not adjusting. Without this level of management, more condors would certainly die.

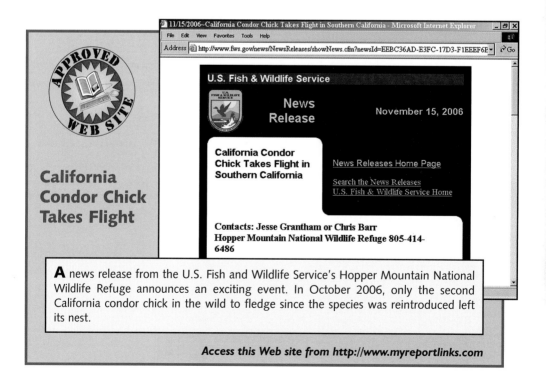

11/15/2006~California Condor Chick Takes Flight in Southern California - Microsoft Internet Explorer

File   Edit   View   Favorites   Tools   Help

Address   http://www.fws.gov/news/NewsReleases/showNews.cfm?newsId=EEBC36AD-E3FC-17D3-F1EEEF6E   Go

U.S. Fish & Wildlife Service

News Release

November 15, 2006

California Condor Chick Takes Flight in Southern California

News Releases Home Page

Search the News Releases
U.S. Fish & Wildlife Service Home

Contacts: Jesse Grantham or Chris Barr
Hopper Mountain National Wildlife Refuge 805-414-6486

APPROVED WEB SITE

California Condor Chick Takes Flight

A news release from the U.S. Fish and Wildlife Service's Hopper Mountain National Wildlife Refuge announces an exciting event. In October 2006, only the second California condor chick in the wild to fledge since the species was reintroduced left its nest.

Access this Web site from http://www.myreportlinks.com

▷ The Return of the Condor to Mexico

In 2002, the efforts to release California condors to another part of their historic range crossed the border. Three condors were released at a site approximately 125 miles (210 kilometers) south

▲ *Condor Chick 412 makes a valiant—and historic—first flight from a remote perch in the Hopper Mountain National Wildlife Refuge. The species' precarious place in our world is symbolized by this young condor's first attempt to fly: cautious success, with a long way to go.*

of the California border, in Sierra San Pedro de Martír National Park. The park is in Baja California, Mexico. This release project is a joint effort of the United States and Mexican governments and nongovernmental organizations from each country.[13]

▶ Flying Free

The autumn of 2006 brought another milestone on the birds' road to recovery. On October 22, California Condor Chick 412, a six-month-old, left its nest in the Hopper Mountain National Wildlife Refuge for the first time. Number 412's first flight was a short one, spanning about fifteen feet, but the chick was seen making more short flights soon afterward. This event marked only the second time that a California condor chick has fledged in the wild in California since the birds were reintroduced in 1992. Steve Thompson, a U.S. Fish and Wildlife manager from the service's California and Nevada office, described why this one chick's first flight is important to the species as a whole: "This is a significant event; each time a condor chick fledges in the wild it brings us that much closer to the goal of the recovery of this great bird."[14]

In 1973, Congress took the farsighted step of creating the Endangered Species Act, widely regarded as the world's strongest and most effective wildlife conservation law. It set an ambitious goal: to reverse the alarming trend of human-caused extinction that threatened the ecosystems we all share.

Each book in this series explores the life of an endangered animal. The books tell how and why the animals have become endangered and explain the efforts being made to restore their populations.

The United States Fish and Wildlife Service and the National Marine Fisheries Service share responsibility for administration of the Endangered Species Act. Over time, animals are added to, reclassified in, or removed from the federal list of Endangered and Threatened Wildlife and Plants. At the time of publication, all the animals in this series were listed as endangered species. The most up-to-date list can be found at **http://www.fws.gov/endangered/wildlife.html**.

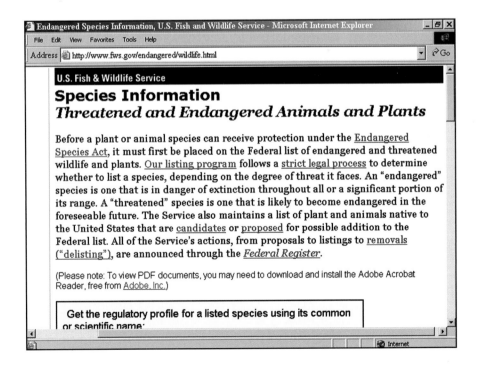

		STOP					
Back	Forward	Stop	Review	Home	Explore	Favorites	History

Report Links

The Internet sites described below can be accessed at http://www.myreportlinks.com

▶**California Condor**
Editor's Choice Learn about the California condor from a wildlife refuge's Web site.

▶**Pinnacles National Monument Condor Program**
Editor's Choice Visit Pinnacles National Monument, a condor release area.

▶**Get the Lead Out**
Editor's Choice Learn about an ongoing—and preventable—threat to released condors.

▶**Oregon Zoo's California Condors**
Editor's Choice View information on the Condor Recovery Program at the Oregon Zoo.

▶**Audubon: California Condor**
Editor's Choice Visit the National Audubon Society's Web site on the California condor.

▶**The Peregrine Fund: California Condor**
Editor's Choice An international conservation fund helps the California condor.

▶**All About Birds: California Condor**
A notable site on birds offers information on the California condor.

▶**Animal Diversity Web: *Gymnogyps californianus***
Learn about the California condor from this university site.

▶**ARKive: California Condor**
View photographs and videos of California condors on this Web site.

▶**California Condor Chick Takes Flight**
Read about only the second California condor chick to fledge in the wild.

▶**California Condor: NPCA**
The National Parks Conservation Association Web site provides information on the California condor.

▶**The California Condor on the Colorado Plateau**
An Arizona university site celebrates the return of the condor.

▶**California's Plants and Animals: California Condor**
Read an historical overview of the California condor.

▶**"The Comeback Condors"**
This site offers an article on the condors' comeback from the brink of extinction.

▶**Condors and Lead**
A state site offers ways hunters can help condors.

Report Links

The Internet sites described below can be accessed at
http://www.myreportlinks.com

▶**Defenders of Wildlife—California Condor**
This Defenders of Wildlife site presents a brief overview of the California condor.

▶**Ecology of Condors**
Learn about the differences and similarities between the condors of North and South America.

▶**eNature: California Condor**
An online field guide presents information on the California condor.

▶**Endangered California Condors: Let Them Eat Seals**
Learn about a study that proposes adding marine mammal carrion to the condors' diet.

▶**"In the Company of Condors"**
A natural-history magazine article recounts the struggle to reintroduce a condor population.

▶**IUCN Red List of Threatened Species**
Read about the California condor's status on the IUCN Red List.

▶**NatureServe Explorer: *Gymnogyps californianus***
Browse through an online encyclopedia to find information about the California condor.

▶**NPR: Saving the California Condor**
Listen to an interview with the author of a book about the California condor success story.

▶**Raptor Center at the University of Minnesota**
A treatment center for birds of prey offers this view of California condors.

▶**San Diego Zoo's Animal Bytes: California Condor**
Find a zoo's overview of the California condor on this site.

▶**USFWS Endangered Species Program Kid's Corner**
This USFWS Web site offers ways you can help save endangered species.

▶**Ventana Wildlife Society Condor Reintroduction**
Learn about the group that reintroduced the California condor to Big Sur, California.

▶**Welcome to the L.A. Zoo—California Condors**
The Web site for one of the four condor breeding facilities offers detailed information.

▶**William L. Finley**
The life of wildlife photographer William L. Finley is profiled on this USFWS site.

▶**Write Your Representative**
Find links to your congressional representatives on this government site.

brood (verb)—To keep eggs and their chicks warm with body heat. Condor parents take turns brooding the egg and the chick. Both parents have a patch of feathers, called a brood patch, on their breast.

chelation—The treatment for lead poisoning in condors. It includes injections twice a day.

clutch—All the eggs in a nest. Condors lay one egg at a time.

critical habitat—Land determined to be necessary for the survival of an endangered species.

crop—A pouch in a condor's esophagus that stores food for digestion later.

double-clutch (verb)—To lay a second egg if something happens to the first one.

fledge (verb)—To learn to fly.

fledgling—A young bird that has just left the nest and learned to fly.

forage (verb)—To move about looking for food.

genes—Molecules that parents pass on to their offspring, which makes them resemble others of their kind. Genes determine the kinds of proteins the young of a species will have. The proteins determine what the offspring will look like and how they will act.

habitat—An area that supports animals and plants by supplying what they need to survive. Condors need high places, such as cliffs, for their nests, and open areas where they can see food. They also need air movement for soaring, and high perches, such as dead branches at the top of tall trees, for roosting.

ornithologist—A scientist who studies birds.

Pleistocene epoch—A time period in Earth's history that began more than 1.5 million years ago and ended about ten thousand years ago.

preening—The method birds use to clean their feathers, usually by pulling the feathers through their beaks.

primary feathers—The feathers on the outside of a bird's wings. These feathers can be spread and maneuvered to control speed and direction.

quill—The hollow shaft of a feather.

regurgitate (verb)—To bring up half-digested food. Condors regurgitate food to feed their chicks.

roost (verb)—To rest on a perch or branch.

scavenger—An animal that only eats food that is already dead. Scavengers do not kill prey. An obligate scavenger is one that is obligated, or restricted, to eating dead animals and will not hunt and kill food.

susceptible—Not resistant to an outside agent or influence.

Chapter 1. A Prehistoric Survivor in Modern Times

1. James Owen, "Seal Meat May Help Save California Condor," *National Geographic.com,* November 8, 2005, <http://news.nationalgeographic.com/news/2005/11/1108_051108_condors.html> (April 17, 2006).

2. John Nielsen, *Condor: To the Brink and Back—The Life and Times of One Giant Bird* (New York: HarperCollins Publishers, 2006), p. 57.

3. "California Condor Recovery," *Arizona Game & Fish,* n.d., <http://www.gf.state.az.us/w_c/california_condor.shtml> (April 27, 2006).

4. Ibid.

Chapter 2. Flying High

1. "Basic Condor," *Hopper Mountain National Wildlife Refuge,* n.d., <http://www.fws.gov/hoppermountain/cacondor/condorbasics.html> (May 28, 2006).

2. John Nielsen, *Condor: To the Brink and Back—The Life and Times of One Giant Bird* (New York: HarperCollins Publishers, 2006), p. 7.

3. Ibid., p. 21.

4. "Animal Bytes," *San Diego Zoo,* n.d., <http://www.sandiegozoo.org/animalbytes/t-condor.html> (April 18, 2006).

5. Noel Snyder and Helen Snyder, *The California Condor* (San Diego: Academic Press, 2000), p. 23.

6. "California Condor Recovery," *Arizona Game & Fish,* n.d., <http://www.gf.state.az.us/w_c/california_condor.shtml> (April 27, 2006).

7. U.S. Fish and Wildlife Service, "California Condor Recovery Plan," Third Revision (Portland, Oreg.: U.S. Fish and Wildlife Service, 1996), p. 8.

8. Ibid., p. 5.

9. Snyder and Snyder, p. 182.

10. U.S. Fish and Wildlife Service, "Endangered and Threatened Wildlife and Plants: Establishment of a Nonessential Experimental Population of California Condors in Northern Arizona," *Federal Register,* vol. 61, no. 201, October 16, 1996, p. 54,045.

11. "California Condors: Facts," *Los Angeles Zoo & Botanical Gardens,* n.d., <http:www.lazoo.org/condorall/facts.html> (June 2, 2006).

12. Snyder and Snyder, pp. 190–191.

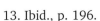

13. Ibid., p. 196.

14. Ibid., pp. 200–201.

15. A.J.S. Rayl, "Becoming a Full-Fledged Condor," *Smithsonian,* vol. 35, no. 6, September 2004, p. 96.

16. Snyder and Snyder, p. 201.

Chapter 3. A Dangerous Environment

1. *Oregon Zoo,* "Oregon Zoo Conservation: Native American History," n.d., <http://www.oregonzoo/Condors/Native American History.htm> (May 29, 2006).

2. Noel Snyder and Helen Snyder, *The California Condor* (San Diego: Academic Press, 2000), p. 44.

3. "Milestones in the History of the California Condor," *Hopper Mountain National Wildlife Refuge,* n.d., <http://www.fws.gov/hoppermountain/cacondor/milestone.html> (May 29, 2006).

4. John Nielsen, *Condor: To the Brink and Back—The Life and Times of One Giant Bird* (New York: HarperCollins Publishers, 2006), p. 83.

5. Ibid., p. 91.

6. Ibid., p. 88.

7. Jane Braxton Little, "Project Gutpile," *Audubon,* December 2002, <http://magazine.audubon.org/features0212/endangered _species.html> (April 28, 2006).

8. Snyder and Snyder, p. 224.

9. U.S. Fish and Wildlife Service, "California Condor Recovery Plan," Third Revision (Portland, Oreg.: U.S. Fish and Wildlife Service, 1996), p. 12.

10. U.S. Fish and Wildlife Service, "California Condor Dies of West Nile Virus," n.d., <http://news.fws.gov/NewsReleases/showNews.cfm?newsId=51307839-65BF-03E7-2AC58AEE6A9F54BC> (May 29, 2006).

Chapter 4. Efforts to Save the California Condor

1. John Nielsen, *Condor: To the Brink and Back—The Life and Times of One Giant Bird* (New York: HarperCollins Publishers, 2006), p. 69.

2. Ibid., pp. 106, 111.

3. Noel Snyder and Helen Snyder, *The California Condor* (San Diego: Academic Press, 2000), p. 65.

4. U.S. Fish and Wildlife Service, "California Condor Recovery Plan," Third Revision (Portland, Oreg.: U.S. Fish and Wildlife Service, 1996), p. 9.

5. Daniel S. Cooper, "Audubon and the California Condor," *Audubon California,* April 2003, <http://www.audubon-ca.org/California_Condor.html> (April 28, 2006).

6. Snyder and Snyder, pp. 84–85.

7. U.S. Fish and Wildlife Service, p. 14.

8. U.S. Fish and Wildlife Service, "Endangered and Threatened Wildlife and Plants: Establishment of a Nonessential Experimental Population of California Condors in Northern Arizona," *Federal Register,* vol. 61, no. 201, October 16, 1996, p. 54,046.

9. Snyder and Snyder, pp. 115–116.

10. U.S. Fish and Wildlife Service, p. 15.

11. Snyder and Snyder, pp. 285, 287.

12. Ibid., p. 293.

13. Cooper.

Chapter 5. Condors in Captivity

1. Susie Kasielke, "Raising California Condors," *Los Angeles Zoo & Botanical Gardens,* 1997, <http://www.lazoo.org/condorall/raise.html> (June 2, 2006).

2. Joy DiGenti, "128th California Condor Hatch at the Wild Animal Park," *San Diego Zoo,* March 20, 2006, <http://www.sandiegozoo.org/wordpress/general/128th-california-condor-hatch-at-the-wild-animal-park/> (May 30, 2006).

3. Noel Snyder and Helen Snyder, *The California Condor* (San Diego: Academic Press, 2000), pp. 289–290.

4. Kasielke.

5. DiGenti.

6. Snyder and Snyder, p. 330.

7. Kasielke.

8. "California Condor Recovery Program," *CRES Projects,* n.d., <http://cres.sandiegozoo.org/projects/sp_condors_recovery_program.html> (May 30, 2006).

9. Katherine Ralls and Jonathan D. Ballou, "Genetic Status and Management of California Condors," *The Condor,* vol. 106, no. 2, May 2004, <http://www.cooper.org/COS/106_2/106_2cont.html> (May 30, 2006).

10. John Nielsen, *Condor: To the Brink and Back—The Life and Times of One Giant Bird* (New York: HarperCollins Publishers, 2006), p. 186.

Chapter 6. Free Again

1. U.S. Fish and Wildlife Service, "California Condor Recovery Plan," Third Revision (Portland, Oreg.: U.S. Fish and Wildlife Service, 1996), p. 17.

2. John Nielsen, *Condor: To the Brink and Back—The Life and Times of One Giant Bird* (New York: HarperCollins Publishers, 2006), p. 184.

3. Daniel S. Cooper, "Audubon and the California Condor," *Audubon California,* April 2003, <http://www.audubon-ca.org/California_Condor.html> (April 28, 2006).

4. Nielsen, p. 209.

5. Ibid., p. 204.

6. A.J.S. Rayl, "Becoming a Full-Fledged Condor," *Smithsonian,* vol. 35, no. 6, September 2004, p. 95.

7. Ibid., p. 95.

8. Noel Snyder and Helen Snyder, *The California Condor* (San Diego: Academic Press, 2000), p. 347.

9. Ibid., p. 344.

10. U.S. Fish and Wildlife Service, "Endangered and Threatened Wildlife and Plants: Establishment of a Nonessential Experimental Population of California Condors in Northern Arizona," *Federal Register,* vol. 61, no. 201, October 16, 1996, p. 54,048.

11. Nielsen, p. 195.

12. Tom J. Cade, Sophie A.H. Osborn, W. Grainger Hunt, and Christopher P. Woods, "Commentary on Released California Condors *Gymnogyps californianus* in Arizona," p. 18, *The Peregrine Fund,* 2004, <http://www.peregrinefund.org/pdfs/condor/condor_paper.pdf> (May 31, 2006).

Chapter 7. Not Yet Wild

1. John Nielsen, *Condor: To the Brink and Back—The Life and Times of One Giant Bird* (New York: HarperCollins Publishers, 2006), p. 241.

2. Ibid., pp. 242–243.

3. A.J.S. Rayl, "Becoming a Full-Fledged Condor," *Smithsonian,* vol. 35, no. 6, September 2004, pp. 96–97.

4. "Breeding Effort and Parental Care in Reintroduced California Condors in the U.S. and Mexico," *CRES Projects,* n.d., <http://cres.sandiegozoo.org/projects/sp_dev_reintro_calif_condors.html> (April 16, 2006).

5. Rayl, p. 96.

6. James Owen, "Seal Meat May Help Save California Condor," *National Geographic.com,* November 8, 2005, <http://news .nationalgeographic.com/news/2005/11/1108_051108_condors .html> (April 17, 2006).

7. Tom J. Cade, Sophie A.H. Osborn, W. Grainger Hunt, and Christopher P. Woods, "Commentary on Released California Condors *Gymnogyps californianus* in Arizona," p. 16, *The Peregrine Fund,* 2004, <http://www.peregrinefund.org/pdfs/condor/condor_paper.pdf> (May 31, 2006).

8. Ibid., pp. 16–17.

9. Jane Braxton Little, "Project Gutpile," *Audubon,* December 2002, <http://magazine.audubon.org/features0212/endangered _species.html> (April 28, 2006).

10. "Lead and Condor Bill Fails to Pass Legislative Committee," *Sacramento Audubon Society,* May 2006, <http://www .sacramentoaudubon.org/newsevent2.htm#AUDUBON% 20CALIFORNIA%20NOTES> (May 31, 2006).

11. *Audubon California, Audubon News,* "Tejon Ranch Bans Lead Ammunition in Move to Help California Condor," February 23, 2007, <http://www.audubon-ca.org/> (March 15, 2007).

12. "California Condor Mortality Challenges," *CRES Projects,* n.d., <http://cres.sandiegozoo.org/projects/sp_dev_reintro_calif_ condors.html> (April 16, 2006).

13. Denise Stockton, "California Condors Return to Mexico," E*ndangered Species Bulletin,* vol. XXVIII, no. 3, May/June 2003.

14. *U.S. Fish and Wildlife Service,* News Release, "California Condor Chick Takes Flight in Southern California," November 15, 2006, <http://www.fws.gov/news/NewsReleases/showNews.cfm ?newsId=EEBC36AD-E3FC-17D3-F1EEEF6BCD8C7611> (January 22, 2007).

Armstrong, Jennifer. *Audubon: Painter of Birds in the Wild Frontier.* New York: H. N. Abrams, 2003.

Becker, John E. *The California Condor.* San Diego: Kidhaven Press, 2004.

Feinstein, Stephen. *California Plants and Animals.* Chicago: Heinemann, 2003.

Gaughen, Shasta. *Endangered Species.* San Diego: Greenhaven Press, 2006.

Hickman, Pamela. *Birds of Prey Rescue: Changing the Future for Endangered Wildlife.* Buffalo: Firefly Books, 2006.

Martin, Patricia A. *California Condors.* New York: Children's Press, 2002.

Miller-Schroeder, Patricia, and Susan Ring. *California Condors.* Chicago: Raintree Publishers, 2004.

Povey, Karen D. *The Condor.* San Diego: Lucent Books, 2001.

Thomas, Peggy. *Bird Alert.* Brookfield, Conn.: Twenty-First Century Books, 2000.

Ward, Adam. *Pocket Factfiles: Endangered Animals.* New York: Sterling Publishing Company, Inc., 2004.